MARKETING AND OPERATIONS MANAGEMENT RESEARCH

MARKET RESEARCH IN THE FEDERAL PROCUREMENT PROCESS

ANALYSIS AND SELECT ASSESSMENTS

MARKETING AND OPERATIONS MANAGEMENT RESEARCH

Additional books in this series can be found on Nova's website under the Series tab.

Additional e-books in this series can be found on Nova's website under the e-book tab.

MARKETING AND OPERATIONS MANAGEMENT RESEARCH

MARKET RESEARCH IN THE FEDERAL PROCUREMENT PROCESS

ANALYSIS AND SELECT ASSESSMENTS

CHERESE HARTELL
EDITOR

NOVINKA

New York

For permission to use material from this book please contact us:
Telephone 631-231-7269; Fax 631-231-8175
Web Site: http://www.novapublishers.com

Additional color graphics may be available in the e-book version of this book.

Library of Congress Cataloging-in-Publication Data

ISBN: 978-1-63482-008-0

Published by Nova Science Publishers, Inc. † New York

CONTENTS

PREFACE

This book assesses selected agencies' market research guidance and policy and how selected agencies conducted market research on selected procurements. It describes the most common elements of the federal procurement process and resources that may be used in that process.

Chapter 1 – The federal government spends hundreds of billions of dollars annually to acquire goods and services from the private sector to support agency missions. Market research—the process used to collect and analyze data about capabilities in the market that satisfy agency needs—is critical to inform decisions about how best to acquire these goods and services.

GAO was asked to examine how federal agencies conduct and use market research. This report assesses (1) selected agencies' market research guidance and policy and (2) how selected agencies conducted market research on selected procurements. GAO reviewed federal regulations and market research policy and guidance at DOD, DHS, and DOT—three agencies GAO selected based on fiscal year 2012 contract obligations and the mix of products and services procured. GAO also reviewed policies and guidance issued by the FAA, which is not subject to the Federal Acquisition Regulation. To assess how market research was conducted on individual contracts, GAO reviewed a nongeneralizable sample of 28 contracts selected based on dollar value and analyzed contract files.

Chapter 2 – This is a memorandum issued by the Office of Management and Budget, Office of Federal Procurement Policy, on "Myth-Busting": Addressing Misconceptions to Improve Communication with Industry during the Acquisition Process, dated Februrary 2, 2011.

Chapter 3 – This is a memorandum issued by the Office of Management and Budget, Office of Federal Procurement Policy, on "Myth-Busting 2":

Addressing Misconceptions and Further Improving Communication with Industry During the Acquisition Process, dated May 7, 2012.

Chapter 4 – In the basic federal procurement process, acquisition personnel, after determining their agency's requirements (that is, the goods and services the agency needs), post a solicitation on the Federal Business Opportunities (FedBizOpps) website. Interested companies prepare their offers in response to the solicitation, and, in accordance with applicable provisions of the Federal Acquisition Regulation (FAR), agency personnel evaluate the offers. Another type of procurement opportunity for a company is to serve as a subcontractor for a government contractor. To be eligible to compete for government contracts, a company must obtain a Data Universal Numbering System (DUNS) number and register with the federal government's System for Award Management (SAM). Several agencies, such as the General Services Administration (GSA), provide assistance and services to existing and potential government contractors. Research and development (R&D) procurement opportunities may involve traditional contracting methods, such as solicitations and contracts, as well as nontraditional methods, which include agency-sponsored contests and venture capital funds.

In: Market Research
Editor: Cherese Hartell
ISBN: 978-1-63482-008-0

Chapter 1

MARKET RESEARCH: BETTER DOCUMENTATION NEEDED TO INFORM FUTURE PROCUREMENTS AT SELECTED AGENCIES*

United States Government Accountability Office

ABBREVIATIONS

CBP	Customs and Border Protection
DHS	Department of Homeland Security
DLA	Defense Logistics Agency
DOD	Department of Defense
DOT	Department of Transportation
FAA	Federal Aviation Administration
FAR	Federal Acquisition Regulation
FHWA	Federal Highway Administration
FPDS-NG	Federal Procurement Database System – Next Generation
OMB	Office of Management and Budget
OPO	Office of Procurement Operations

* This is an edited, reformatted and augmented version of The United States Government Accountability Office publication, GAO-15-8, dated October 2014.

Why GAO Did This Study

The federal government spends hundreds of billions of dollars annually to acquire goods and services from the private sector to support agency missions. Market research—the process used to collect and analyze data about capabilities in the market that satisfy agency needs—is critical to inform decisions about how best to acquire these goods and services.

GAO was asked to examine how federal agencies conduct and use market research. This report assesses (1) selected agencies' market research guidance and policy and (2) how selected agencies conducted market research on selected procurements. GAO reviewed federal regulations and market research policy and guidance at DOD, DHS, and DOT—three agencies GAO selected based on fiscal year 2012 contract obligations and the mix of products and services procured. GAO also reviewed policies and guidance issued by the FAA, which is not subject to the Federal Acquisition Regulation. To assess how market research was conducted on individual contracts, GAO reviewed a nongeneralizable sample of 28 contracts selected based on dollar value and analyzed contract files.

What GAO Recommends

To inform future acquisitions, GAO recommends that the Secretary of Transportation update its market research guidance and the Secretaries of Defense and Homeland Security take action to ensure their acquisition personnel clearly document the basic elements of the market research that was conducted. The agencies concurred with these recommendations.

What GAO Found

Market research guidance at the Departments of Defense (DOD), Homeland Security (DHS), and Transportation (DOT) and the Federal Aviation Administration (FAA) is consistent with federal regulations in terms of market research objectives and builds on the techniques for communicating with industry outlined in federal regulations. All four agencies require that market research be clearly documented and note that documentation can inform current and future procurements. GAO found, however, that the agencies' guidance varied on the specificity of market research documentation. For example, DOD, DHS, and FAA guidance identify specific market research elements to be documented. Based on analysis of these market research elements, GAO identified four elements which, if recorded, would provide an understanding of the research completed. These elements include the market research methods used, when it was conducted, an analysis of vendor capabilities, and a conclusion. DOT's market research guidance did not require specific elements to be documented, which increases the risk that it would not be available to inform future procurements.

All 28 contracts GAO reviewed included some evidence of the market research conducted. The market research conducted on the 12 higher dollar contracts GAO reviewed tended to be more robust and include more techniques that involved outreach to vendors—such as issuing requests for information to industry—which appeared to help promote competition. Agencies did not take advantage of many available market research techniques on the 16 lower dollar contracts GAO reviewed and as a result may have missed opportunities to promote competition.

GAO also identified limitations in the market research for seven DOD and DHS lower dollar contracts that appeared to be incomplete or outdated. For example, DHS relied on incomplete information regarding potential vendors' ability to meet its requirement for parking services. Further, in 14 of the 28 contracts, the four agencies did not document one or more of four basic elements that GAO's review of agency guidance identified as important to the ability to understand the research. GAO identified this shortfall most often on lower dollar contracts reviewed at DOD and DHS. Internal control standards state that significant events need to be clearly documented so as to ensure management directives are carried out. Not documenting basic elements of the market research potentially limits the ability of agency acquisition personnel to use market research to inform future procurements, a goal identified in agency guidance.

* * *

October 9, 2014

The Honorable Claire McCaskill
Chairman

The Honorable Ron Johnson
Ranking Member
Subcommittee on Financial and Contracting Oversight
Committee on Homeland Security and Governmental Affairs
United States Senate

The federal government spends hundreds of billions of dollars each year to acquire goods and services through the commercial marketplace to enable agencies to fulfill their missions. These needs range from simple goods readily available in the marketplace, such as office supplies, to services such as janitorial services, to complex goods and services such as information technology systems. Market research—the process used to collect and analyze data about capabilities in the market that could satisfy an agency's needs—is a critical step in the acquisition process, informing key decisions about how best to acquire goods and services. For example, effective market research can help agencies determine the availability of vendors to satisfy requirements; knowledge of marketplace suppliers and prices can be critical to the government's ability to negotiate a good deal and foster competition. On the other hand, poor market research techniques could lessen the government's ability to achieve competition and negotiate fair and reasonable prices.

You asked us to assess how federal agencies are conducting and using market research. This report assesses (1) selected agencies' guidance and policy on market research and (2) how selected agencies conducted market research on selected procurements. To assess agency guidance and policy on market research, we reviewed and identified criteria for the conduct and use of market research in government-wide regulations and policy, such as the Federal Acquisition Regulation (FAR), including FAR Subpart 7.1—Acquisition Plans and FAR Part 10—Market Research, and Office of Management and Budget (OMB) memorandums related to market research.[1] To assess specific agency guidance and policy and to illustrate how market research is performed at agencies of various sizes and that procure a range of products and services, we selected three departments for the review—the Department of Defense (DOD), the Department of Homeland Security (DHS) and the Department of Transportation (DOT). We selected these departments based on fiscal year 2012 contract obligations—the most recent fiscal year of information available when we started our review—and to get a good mix of products and services procured. Within each department, we selected two components for further review—DOD's Department of the Army and Defense Logistics Agency (DLA); DHS's Office of Procurement Operations (OPO)[2] and U.S. Customs and Border Protection (CBP); and DOT's Federal Aviation Administration (FAA) and Federal Highway Administration (FHWA)—based primarily on their fiscal year 2012 obligations. For each department and component, we reviewed guidance and policy related to market research, including agency supplements to the FAR, market research guides and templates, and policy memorandums that reference market research, such as DOD's Better Buying Power policy memorandums. Key agency guidance reviewed included DOD's Defense Standardization Program, Market Research: Gathering Information about Commercial Products and Services, SD-5; DHS's Market Research Guide; DOT's Market Research Guide, Acquisition Policy DOT Dash 2010-11; and FAA's Procurement Guidance T3.2.1.2—Market Analysis.[3] Since the FAR and DOT acquisition regulation do not apply to FAA acquisitions, we analyzed FAA policy and guidance separately from DOT.[4] We interviewed senior acquisition officials at each department to develop a better understanding of agency policies and component guidance related to market research and to identify agency initiatives related to market research.

To examine how agencies conducted market research on selected procurements, we used the Federal Procurement Data System-Next Generation (FPDS-NG) to select a nongeneralizable sample of 30 contracts awarded in fiscal year 2012 with contract dollar values of at least $500,000 from the six components within DOD, DHS, and DOT. We selected this threshold as the contracts above this threshold represented more than 92 percent of contract dollars awarded in fiscal year 2012 at each component reviewed. Within each selected agency component, we created randomized lists of fiscal year 2012 contracts within two strata— (1) contracts valued at more than $10 million and (2) contracts valued between $500,000 and $10 million. The higher dollar stratum represented the greatest portion of contract dollars awarded in fiscal year 2012 within each component—ranging between 79 percent and 98 percent of dollars, while the lower dollar stratum represented a larger portion of contract actions awarded in fiscal year 2012. Within each stratum, we selected a nongeneralizable sample of contracts to obtain, to the extent possible, a mix of products and services and a mix of competed and noncompeted contracts within each component. We selected two contracts from the first stratum and three from the second stratum (five per component) from the randomized lists for each component. Overall, we selected 30 contracts for a more in-depth review. We excluded 2 of the 30 selected contracts from our final analysis—1 from FHWA and one from FAA—because, as of July 31, 2014, we were unable to assess the market research for those contracts due to missing market research documentation and staff changes since the award of the contracts.[5] As a result, our analysis in this report is based on 28 selected contracts. For each contract, we reviewed contract documents related to market research, including market research reports, acquisition plans, justifications and approvals for sole-source awards, price negotiation memorandums and independent government cost estimates, and interviewed or obtained information from cognizant contracting and program officials. The findings from our selected contracts are not generalizable to the population of all contracts within the selected agencies or components.

To assess the reliability of the FPDS-NG data used to select the contracts for review, we compared key data elements from FPDS-NG to the contract documentation, including the contract number, agency name, and whether or not the contract had been competed using full and open competition. Where we found discrepancies relevant to our methodology, we made adjustments to maintain the integrity of our selection criteria. For example, we excluded 7 contracts because the contracts were miscoded in FPDS-NG and therefore should have been excluded from our sample. Specifically, we excluded 5 contracts because they were small business set asides, 1 contract because the total dollar value fell below the $500,000 threshold for inclusion in the review, and 1 contract because it was a research and development contract. Because we had randomized lists of contracts for each of the components, we replaced the miscoded contracts with another contract. Once we corrected for these errors, we concluded the data obtained was sufficiently reliable for the purposes of this report.

Market research serves several purposes, including identifying sources capable of meeting the government's need, promoting competition, identifying whether commercial items can meet the government's needs, and identifying whether small businesses are capable of meeting the requirement. For the purposes of our review, we focused our work on how market research informed the competition strategy and the contracting officer's analysis of price reasonableness. We did not assess how market research informed the small business determination or how it informed the decision to use a commercial item given GAO has prior work that focuses on these issues.[6] Appendix I provides additional details on our scope and methodology.

We conducted this performance audit from August 2013 to October 2014 in accordance with generally accepted government auditing standards. Those standards require that we plan and perform the audit to obtain sufficient, appropriate evidence to provide a reasonable basis for our findings and conclusions based on our audit objectives. We believe that the evidence obtained provides a reasonable basis for our findings and conclusions based on our audit objectives.

BACKGROUND

Market research has been a statutory requirement since the passage of the Competition in Contracting Act of 1984, which required the use of market research and acquisition planning, and solicitation of proposals, to obtain competition.[7] The FAR defines market research as the process used to collect and analyze data about capabilities in the market that could satisfy an agency's procurement needs. The FAR provides general policies and procedures for conducting market research with the goal of arriving at the most suitable approach to acquiring, distributing, and supporting supplies and services.[8]

Market research is conducted throughout various phases of an acquisition, and involves the program office and the contracting office. The program office typically starts the market research in the acquisition planning phase once a need is identified. The program office may then contact its contracting office to coordinate the development of key acquisition documents. The program office is primarily responsible for conducting market research in the early phases of an acquisition and submitting a formal request for contract to the contracting office. Responsibility for market research shifts from the program office to the contracting office as the acquisition process progresses (see figure 1). Further, the FAR requires that market research be conducted, appropriate to the circumstances, before developing new requirements documents. In addition, the FAR identifies a number of other points in the acquisition process when market research must be conducted, including prior to soliciting offers for contracts above the simplified acquisition threshold and below this threshold if adequate information is not available and circumstances justify its cost.[9]

Federal regulations provide some flexibility in terms of how and to what extent market research should be conducted, considering the nature of the procurement. Specifically, the FAR provides that the extent of market research depends on a number of factors, such as urgency, estimated dollar value, complexity, and past experience.[10] The FAR also states that agencies should document the results of market research in a manner appropriate to the size and complexity of the acquisition, but does not prescribe any particular format or specific elements for documentation.

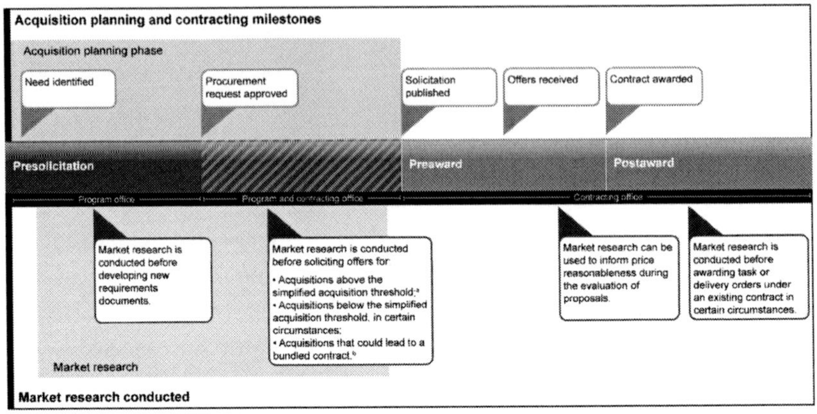

Source: GAO analysis of federal regulations and agency guidance. | GAO-15-8

Source: GAO analysis of federal regulations and agency guidance| GAO-15-8.

[a] The simplified acquisition threshold is generally $150,000.

[b] Bundling refers to the consolidating of two or more requirements for goods or services previously provided or performed under separate smaller contracts into a solicitation for a single contract that is likely to be unsuitable for award to a small business concern.

Figure 1. Market Research and the Acquisition Process.

We have issued a number of reports with implications for market research. In our 2011 report on acquisition planning, we note that market research is a part of the acquisition planning process, a process that is responsible for successful acquisition outcomes.[11] In addition, we issued several reports related to the market research objective of promoting competition. For example, in a January 2012 report reviewing DOD's use of the national security exception (which allows agencies to limit competition for a contract in instances when disclosure of an agency's needs would compromise national security), as well as in a March 2013 report reviewing DOD's use of competitive procedures, we found few details about the market research findings that helped justify the decision to pursue a noncompetitive or limited competition award for some contracts reviewed.[12] In contrast, our best practices work has shown how market research can be used to enhance competition. Specifically, in an April 2013 report identifying leading commercial company practices for acquiring services, we reported that one company sometimes chose to execute a short term contract to buy time if market research showed a more competitive deal could be obtained at a later date.[13]

While market research is one factor that may affect competition, there are a number of other factors as well, such as whether the government owns the rights to the technical data on a contract and the relationship between a program office and a contracting office. For example, in a May 2014 report reviewing DOD's noncompetitive and one-offer awards, we found that the justifications for half of the noncompetitive contracts and task orders stated that the awards could not be competed due to a lack of technical data.[14] Similarly, in a March 2014 report reviewing the use of the unusual and compelling urgency exception to full and open competition at three federal agencies, we found that for 10 DOD contracts reviewed, the government was unable to compete requirements in part because of a lack of access to technical data packages or proprietary data.[15] In terms of the relationship between the contracting and program offices, in July 2010 we reported that several agencies recognized that program offices place pressure on the contracting process to award new contracts to a specific vendor without competition. Further, we reported that many contracting officials we spoke with recognized that program staff sometimes prefer a specific vendor—often an incumbent—in some cases because a relationship has developed between the program office and the contractor, who understands the program requirements.[16] We also found that a strong incumbent, sometimes coupled with overly restrictive government requirements, are factors that may contribute to receiving only one offer on a competitive procurement.

SELECTED AGENCIES' MARKET RESEARCH GUIDANCE IS GENERALLY CONSISTENT WITH FEDERAL REGULATIONS, BUT DOCUMENTATION REQUIREMENTS VARY AT SOME AGENCIES

We found that agencies' market research guidance at DOD, DHS, DOT, and FAA is consistent with federal regulations in terms of market research objectives, techniques, and documentation, but agencies' guidance varies from one another on the specificity of documentation required. For example, DHS guidance requires that specific elements of market research be documented and DOD and FAA make recommendations on the types of elements to be documented. In contrast, DOT provides acquisition staff limited instruction, stating that the level of detail might vary based on factors such as whether the market research is for a onetime or recurring requirement but its market research guidance does not require any specific elements to be documented. Based on our review of agencies' market research guidance, we identified four basic market research elements, which, if recorded, would allow those not connected with the research to understand how the acquisition team collected and analyzed information about capabilities within the market to satisfy agency needs. These four market research elements include (1) the methods used, (2) the timeframes when staff used them, (3) an analysis of the capabilities of potential sources, and (4) a conclusion based on this analysis.

Selected Agencies' Guidance Is Consistent with FAR Objectives for Market Research and Provides Additional Techniques for Communicating with the Industry

Our analysis found that, consistent with the FAR, selected agencies' guidance indicates that market research may be used to inform two key decisions. The first decision—deciding whether or not to conduct a full and open competition—is made as part of the acquisition planning process and one of the purposes of market research is to promote competition to the maximum extent practicable.[17] Federal regulations require agencies to perform acquisition planning activities for all acquisitions to ensure that the government meets its needs in the most effective, economical, and timely manner possible.[18] The second decision—deciding whether the prices to be paid for the goods or services is reasonable—is made prior to the award of a contract. This decision is commonly referred to as the "price reasonableness" decision. While not required, the FAR identifies market research as a method for this purpose.[19] More specific information about the FAR provisions and how agency guidance reinforces them follows:

- Competition: The FAR requires, among other things, that market research and acquisition planning be used to promote and provide for full and open competition or, if not required, to obtain competition to the maximum extent practicable.[20] Agencies' guidance reinforces the goal of providing for competition in several ways, for example, by instructing acquisition staff to identify and analyze the capabilities of potential sources prior to making the competition decision, which would include determining whether thc requirement should be set aside for small business concerns, open to full and open competition, or sole-sourced to a specific vendor.[21] DOD and DOT guidance explains that market research helps the acquisition team become informed consumers, enabling the team to develop the optimal procurement strategy. DHS guidance notes that market research should be used to refine requirements to maximize the benefit of competitive market forces, as needed, and to consider if modifying a requirement may allow a commercial, rather than a noncommercial, item to be acquired.

- Price Reasonableness: The FAR identifies the comparison of proposed prices on a contract with prices obtained through market research for the same or similar items as one of several methods for determining price reasonableness.[22] Agencies' guidance confirms the usefulness of market research in informing what price would be reasonable for the government to pay for a procurement. For example, FAA guidance states that market research and analysis can help ensure that the government's needs are met in a cost effective manner based on understanding prices in the commercial marketplace. DOD guidance similarly explains that knowledge of market pricing information is necessary for planning for contract obligations and determining price reasonableness.

Agencies' guidance builds upon the market research techniques identified in the FAR by identifying a greater variety of ways of communicating with industry and emphasizing the importance of doing so. [23] The market research techniques described in the FAR, as well as those in agencies' guidance, can be broadly categorized as those used by acquisition staff to (1) obtain information from internal sources, such as reviewing the results of recent market research undertaken to meet similar or identical requirements, or (2) communicate directly with external sources, particularly industry sources (see table 1).

Table 1. Market Research Techniques Identified Under Part 10 of the Federal Acquisition Regulation (FAR) and in Agency Guidance

	FAR	*DOD*	*DHS*	*DOT*	*FAA*
Internal Information					
Reviewing the results of recent market research undertaken to meet similar or identical requirements	√	√	√	√	√

Table 1. (Continued)

	FAR	*DOD*	*DHS*	*DOT*	*FAA*
Contacting knowledgeable government officials on market capabilities to meet requirements, including obtaining source lists of similar items from other contracting activities or agencies	√	√	√	√	√
Querying the government-wide database of contracts and other procurement instruments intended for use by multiple agencies available at www.contractdirectory.gov/contractdirectory/ and other government and commercial databases	√	√	√	√	√
Reviewing catalogs and other generally available product literature published by manufacturers, distributors, and dealers or available on-line	√	√	√	√	√
Reviewing prior acquisition history			√		
External Information					
Contacting knowledgeable industry officials on market capabilities to meet requirements or obtaining source lists of similar items from trade associations or other sources	√	√	√	√	√
Conducting interchange meetings or holding presolicitation conferences to involve potential offerors early in the acquisition process	√	√	√	√	√
Publishing formal requests for information in appropriate technical or scientific journals or business publications	√	√	√	√	√
Participating in interactive, on-line communication among industry, acquisition personnel, and customers	√		√		√
Holding one-on-one meetings with industry		√	√	√	√
Publishing requests for information or sources sought notices at www.FedBizOpps.gov[a]		√	√	√	
Attending trade fairs and conferences		√	√	√	
Performing site visits (program staff visiting vendors or vendors visiting the agency)		√	√	√	
Preparing a formal survey or questionnaire and sending it to multiple suppliers		√	√		√
Sponsoring industry conferences or industry days		√	√		

Source: GAO analysis of part 10 of the FAR and of agency guidance. | GAO-15-8

[a] Federal Business Opportunities, commonly referred to as FedBizOpps, is a web-based government portal which allows all potential vendors to consider federal procurement opportunities.

Agencies' guidance generally mirrors the FAR in terms of potential internal techniques that could be used to conduct market research and provides additional means to communicate with industry that are not specified in the FAR. For example, while the FAR suggests that acquisition staff place a request for information in technical or scientific journals or business publications, DOD, DHS, and DOT guidance expands upon this suggestion by indicating that requests for information could be posted on FedBizOpps. A contracting officer could use such a posting to solicit industry response to a questionnaire or obtain industry comment on a draft statement of work on behalf of an acquisition team. Further, a contracting officer can post a sources sought notice—a notice requesting that vendors interested in providing a particular product or service identify themselves—on FedBizOpps. DHS guidance notes that vendors who respond to the notice usually describe their capabilities or similar projects they have conducted, among other things. While DOD guidance also recommends these techniques, it also suggests that acquisition staff take additional measures to reach vendors that have not previously bid on government contracts, such as advertising in business publications. In addition, DOD guidance recommends attending trade shows and conferences as a good source of general information about an industry and DHS guidance identifies these events as places to meet industry leaders and vendors.

To promote industry outreach, each agency in our review has developed guidance, known as vendor communication plans, designed to facilitate interaction between acquisition staff and vendors. Agencies' actions were consistent with an OMB initiative intended to encourage acquisition staff to have productive interactions with industry partners during the acquisition process.[24] In a February 2, 2011 memorandum, OMB stated that such outreach is important so that the government has a clear understanding of the marketplace and can award a contract for an effective solution at a reasonable price.[25] The memorandum further states that acquisition staff were not taking full advantage of flexibilities offered in the FAR because of their concern that vendors could misinterpret the discussions as obligating the government to conduct business with them and that agencies must remove unnecessary barriers to reasonable communication with industry. DOD and DHS guidance cite the importance of clear and frequent communication between government and industry because of benefits for improved acquisition outcomes, including opening the door for more small business participation.

While agencies' guidance identifies a broad array of market research techniques, the guidance also notes that the extent or type of market research will vary, depending on factors including urgency, estimated dollar value, complexity, and past experience. For example, DHS guidance notes that several methods of obtaining information from industry, such as sponsoring presolicitation conferences to discuss industry comments on proposed solicitations, are conducted more typically for complex requirements. DOD guidance recognizes the importance of market research on lower dollar procurements, noting that DOD awards a multitude of lower-dollar contracts for new products or services and that the goals of market research to understand the commercial market remain the same for these procurements. DOD and DOT guidance suggests that acquisition staff weigh the administrative cost of conducting market research to the potential benefits. Similarly, DHS guidance suggests that the acquisition team solicit the contracting officer's advice to avoid requesting more than the minimum information necessary from potential sources when conducting market research. FAA guidance suggests that market research may range from a telephone call to formal market surveys or solicitations requesting information.

Selected Agencies Require Market Research Be Documented, but Vary in the Amount of Specific Information Required

All four agencies require that market research be clearly documented since it can inform current and future procurements, but the guidance varies in terms of the elements that are to be included in the documentation. The FAR requires that for more complex and higher dollar procurements, acquisition personnel prepare written acquisition plans that include a description of prospective sources and address the extent and results of market research and the impact of these findings on various elements of the plan.[26] Consistent with the FAR, all of the agencies in our review have guidance regarding acquisition planning for procurements designated as more complex or higher value. At DOD, DHS, and DOT, written acquisition plans are typically required for higher valued acquisitions. For example, at DHS, these plans are typically required for acquisitions of $10 million and above and, at DOT, written acquisition plans are generally required for procurements greater than $20 million. FAA has similar requirements for acquisition plans for most procurements greater than $25,000. In addition, in most cases where a product or service is to be acquired on a sole-source basis, the FAR requires that contracting officers prepare a written justification, also known as a justification for other than full and open competition, which is to include a description of the market research conducted or the reason that market research was not conducted as a part of justifying that a contract be solesourced.[27] The agencies in our review all have guidance regarding justifications for sole-source contracts, and DHS and FAA's guidance specifically address the requirement to describe the market research in support of the sole-source award.

Beyond the market research information required as part of acquisition plans for more complex, higher dollar value procurements, or as part of the justification and approval for sole-source procurements, we found that the specific type of market research information that must be documented for all procurements, including contracts of lower value, varies considerably by agency. Only DHS required, as of January 2014, that specific elements—such as who conducted the market research, the methods used, and the outcome and impact of the market research—be documented. In contrast, DOD, DOT, and FAA do not require that specific elements be recorded consistently, although DOD and FAA guidance contain recommendations on elements that could be recorded (see figure 2).

Agency	Specific elements are required by policy	Specific elements are recommended in guidance or template
Department of Defense		✓
Department of Homeland Security	✓	✓
Department of Transportation		
Federal Aviation Administration		✓

Required Elements at DHS
Department of Homeland Security Acquisition Manual:
A market research report is required for contract actions awarded above the simplified acquisition threshold and shall provide, at a minimum, the following information:[a]

1. Participants in the market research effort and responsibilities of team members;
2. Market research methods used; and
3. Outcome of the market research identifying potential sources and findings that impact the procurement.

Source: GAO analysis of DOD, DHS, DOT and FAA guidance.| GAO-15-8.
[a] The simplified acquisition threshold is generally $150,000.

Figure 2. Required and Recommended Market Research Elements as of July 2014.

DOD and FAA market research guidance recommends, but does not require, documenting elements similar to the ones DHS requires be documented. In addition, DOD guidance recommends documenting the timeframes during which the market research was conducted, a description of commercial business practices, and related cost and price factors. DOD, DHS, and FAA provide templates or sample memorandums for the contract file that contain placeholders for recommended information.[28] DOT market research guidance does not specify elements to be documented, and notes that the type and amount of information to be kept should be based on how it may be used in the future and whether the documentation is for a one-time, unique, or recurring requirement.

DOD, DHS, and FAA have taken steps to enhance the documentation of market research information over the past few years. For example:

- In April 2012, DOD officials issued a template, including recommended information, for preparing market research reports for services acquisitions. The template was prepared by a working group that identified best practices for conducting and documenting market research to allow for more effective collection and sharing of market research across DOD. The first part of the template is for recording basic information, such as a description of vendor capabilities and small business opportunities. The second part of the template is targeted toward more complex high-dollar value procurements and requires more detailed information about the commercial market, such as a description of the demand for the service and an assessment of fair and reasonable prices. DOD officials reported to us that they are considering whether use of the template should be mandatory.
- In October 2012, FAA issued its sample Market Research Memorandum to the File with recommended elements to record, and in April 2013, FAA first required the use of written acquisition plans. The acquisition plan template for acquisitions above the simplified acquisition threshold instructs that the results of market research be recorded, as well as the size and status of each source, and a competition determination—for example, whether the work should be set aside for small businesses.
- DHS had previously included in guidance that minimum elements be documented. In January 2014 DHS incorporated these required elements into the Department of Homeland Security Acquisition Manual. According to DHS officials, by doing so, the agency elevated the importance of including these elements in market research reports.

Based on our analysis of market research elements identified in DOD, DHS, and FAA policy, guidance, or templates, we identified and discussed with agencies' officials four basic market research elements, which, if recorded, would allow those not connected with the research to understand how the acquisition team collected and analyzed information about capabilities within the market to satisfy agency needs. These four market research elements include (1) the methods used, (2) the timeframes when staff used them, (3) an analysis of the capabilities of potential sources, and (4) a conclusion based on this analysis. DOD, DHS, and FAA market research policies, guidance, or templates included at least three of the four basic elements. For example, at DHS, three of these elements were included in the Department of Homeland Security Acquisition Manual and the fourth element, timeframes, was included in DHS's market research template. However, DOT's market research guidance did not include any specific elements. Internal control standards state that control activities, such as policies and procedures, help ensure that management directives are carried out and actions are taken to address risks.[29] Requiring that specific market research elements be documented in contract files would help ensure that documentation is readily available to inform current and future procurements.

Selected Agencies May Have Missed Opportunities to Promote Competition and Inform Future Procurements on Lower Dollar Contracts

We found that all 28 contracts we reviewed included some evidence of market research, but the market research on higher dollar value contracts—those valued at $10 million or more—tended to be more robust and appeared to help promote competition. Agencies did not take advantage of many available market research techniques on lower dollar value contracts, and as a result may have missed opportunities to promote competition. In 10 of the 12 higher dollar contracts we reviewed, agency officials conducted outreach to vendors through issuance of requests for information, draft requests for proposals, or other techniques. In some cases, this approach resulted in the agency modifying or clarifying its requirements to encourage competition, and all but one of the higher dollar contracts that conducted some type of formal outreach to industry received more than one offer. In contrast, in only 4 of the 16 lower dollar contracts did DOD, DHS, and DOT officials conduct formal outreach to industry, instead often relying on issuance of a notice that the agency intended to award a contract on a sole-source basis or on a review of the government's acquisition history. In several cases, DOD and DHS officials relied on market research that appeared to be incomplete or outdated. Overall, we identified limitations in the market research supporting seven lower dollar value contracts, all of which were sole-sourced or received only one offer. Similarly, while all 28 contracts we reviewed contained evidence of market research, agency officials often did not document one or more of the four basic market research elements which we identified based on our review of agencies' guidance, potentially limiting the ability to use this market research to inform future procurements. We also found that agencies' officials used market research to inform price reasonableness determinations in most of the contracts we reviewed, though other techniques were also frequently used to inform pricing determinations.

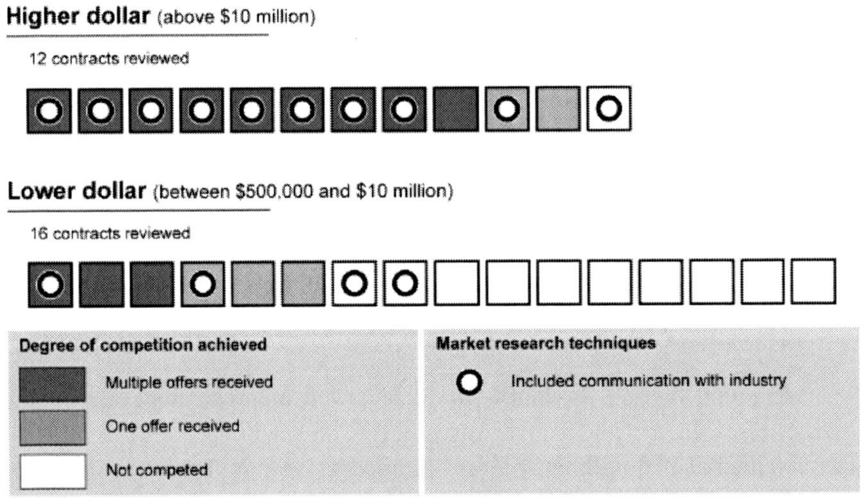

Source: GAO analysis of DOD, DHS, DOT and FAA documentation.| GAO-15-8.

Note: For the purposes of this analysis, we defined communication with industry to include attending industry trade shows or conducting site visits, contacting multiple potential vendors and using their feedback to update or clarify the requirement, or publishing formal requests for information, sources sought notices, or draft solicitations in FedBizOpps.

Figure 3. Market Research Techniques and Competition Results on 28 Contracts GAO Reviewed.

Market Research on Higher Dollar Value Contracts Involved More Communication with Industry and Contributed to Competition

We found that agencies' market research on the higher dollar value contracts generally involved more communication with industry and these contracts were more often awarded on a competitive basis than were the lower dollar value contracts we reviewed (see figure 3).

In particular, we found that for higher dollar contracts, agencies' officials made more extensive use of techniques involving communication with industry, such as issuing requests for information and draft requests for proposals, and holding conferences with vendors—using these types of techniques on 10 of the 12 higher dollar value contracts we reviewed. These methods allowed agencies' officials to gather vendor feedback and collect information that could be used to refine requirements and inform competition determinations. The lower dollar contracts we reviewed relied more extensively on internal sources of information, such as the knowledge of program officials, examinations of acquisition history, or on the issuance of notices of intent to sole-source as the main sources of market research, rather than on formal outreach to industry.[30] Specifically, while market research on 4 of the 16 lower dollar contracts we reviewed involved outreach to industry, there was no outreach to industry on the other 12 contracts reviewed. The FAR states that agencies are encouraged to promote early exchanges of information about future acquisitions to, among other things, improve the understanding of the government's requirement and industry capabilities.

The following examples highlight some market research techniques used by agencies' officials on higher dollar value contracts, conclusions reached based on the market research, and competition outcomes:

- The FAA awarded a $2 billion contract for data communication integrated services after conducting 14 formal requests for information and other outreach to potential vendors over a 4-year period. The contracting staff used the information gathered from industry to help develop the final requirement. FAA received offers from three vendors it had identified as likely to make offers based on its market research efforts.
- Similarly, on an $87 million DHS contract for guard services, the contracting specialist identified thousands of potential contractors through a database, narrowed this number to 172 potential vendors by

cross referencing the vendor information with online information about vendors with existing government-wide contracts, issued a sources sought notice, evaluated 26 responses to the notice, and ultimately concluded that there were enough sources capable of meeting the need to allow for full and open competition. Eighteen vendors made offers on the contract.

- In a $72 million DHS acquisition for program management and logistics support, a total of 31 contractors responded to either a request for information posted in 2009 and/or a subsequent one posted in 2011. The feedback obtained through the requests for information led to the conclusion that the acquisition strategy should be revised to address industry questions, comments, and concerns, including issues with funding and performance related to the contract structure. Agency officials therefore issued a sole-source bridge contract, in part so that they could revise the requirement. Additionally, the market research report for this contract stated that while all 31 contractors responding to the requests for information might not make offers or be capable of fulfilling the requirement, the information gathered from the responses gave the agency insight into the capabilities of the marketplace, and led to the conclusion that there would be ample qualified vendors in the market to meet the requirements of a subsequent contract. According to an agency official, the award of the follow-on contract is now in process—being competed among certain small business set aside vendors—and the agency has received multiple offers. The offers are currently being evaluated, and DHS officials anticipate awarding the contract around the close of fiscal year 2014.

Overall, our work found the market research, and in particular, industry outreach efforts, appeared to contribute to the degree of competition achieved on the higher dollar contracts we reviewed. For example, 9 of the 12 higher dollar contracts we reviewed received more than one offer; and in all but one of these cases, agencies' officials conducted some type of formal outreach efforts to industry.

While the higher dollar value contracts tended to be competed and most involved outreach with industry, we found additional market research actions could have potentially promoted competition on a 3-year, $210 million DLA contract for tax-free fuel in Italy awarded in 2011. In this case, DLA enables U.S. military personnel to purchase fuel on a tax-free basis while stationed there. To do so, DLA issued a solicitation that required potential offerors, among other things, to (1) have at least 1,000 service stations in Italy and (2) be able to accept printed coupons that allowed military personnel to buy the fuel on a tax-free basis. The market research performed by program officials consisted of a list of all of the fuel companies operating in Italy; however, contracting officials confirmed that only two of the nine companies on the list were likely to be able to meet the requirement of 1,000 gas stations included in the solicitation. Both of these companies were incumbents on the prior contract. However, contracting officials stated that one of the two companies, which was an incumbent, did not submit an offer because the continued use of printed coupons was too cumbersome for them. After receiving a single offer, the contracting officer asked the program office whether it was feasible to use a credit card program or a combination of printed coupons and credit cards to meet the need, as agency officials stated that DLA has done in other countries, but the requirement was left unchanged and the contract was awarded to the single vendor that submitted an offer. Contracting officials told us that as of May 2014, they were considering developing a business case analysis to assess the costs and benefits of switching to a credit card program. DLA officials told us that formally analyzing alternative approaches and changing from a coupon to a credit card program would need to be coordinated through the Italian government since tax-free privileges are a benefit provided by the Italian government.

Market Research on Lower Dollar Value Contracts Was Often Limited and May Have Missed Opportunities to Promote Competition

Lower dollar value contracts we selected were less likely to be competed than higher dollar value contracts—while 6 of the 16 lower dollar value contracts were competed, 3 of those received only one offer, and the other 10 contracts were sole-sourced. As noted previously, market research is to be used to promote and provide for full and open competition or, when not required, to obtain competition to the maximum extent practicable. Even in situations when agency officials anticipate awarding a sole-source contract, the contracting officer is generally required to identify actions, if any, the agency may take to remove or overcome any barriers to competition for future acquisitions of the supplies or services required. Overall, we identified limitations in the market research supporting seven lower dollar value contracts awarded by DOD and DHS, all of which were sole-sourced or received only one offer. As a result, DOD and DHS officials may have missed opportunities to promote competition. In several cases, agency officials relied on market research that appeared to be incomplete or outdated. Examples of these cases are highlighted below:

- Market research on a $1.6 million DHS contract to rent parking spaces near a DHS building located in Arlington, Virginia, cited multiple potential vendors through a review of prior acquisition history, a government database, and a DHS source list, but the market research did not include any formal outreach to industry. The market research, conducted by a program official, identified three potential parking facilities within one block of the DHS building but did not assess whether potential vendors could provide direct elevator access to the building, a key requirement specifically included in the solicitation. The agency received only one offer from a parking facility adjacent to the building. Subsequently, an agency attorney who reviewed the scope of work wrote that the requirements seemed unusually narrow and that only one vendor would likely be able to provide a parking garage with an elevator that connected to the office building. We found no evidence that DHS used market research to reassess whether DHS's requirement could be modified, and as a result, the agency may have missed opportunities to receive more than one offer.
- In a $2 million Army contract for flight simulator training services receiving only one offer, the primary market research was a sources sought notice posted for 10 days on FedBizOpps for which a response was only received from the incumbent vendor. Further, over a 10-year procurement history for these services, market research consisted of two sources sought notices—the one already discussed and one issued in 2006. While the contracting officer doubted whether any other vendors had the capability to fulfill this particular requirement, the contracting officer acknowledged more market research could have been done to ensure this conclusion was accurate, such as outreach to other potential vendors who provide flight simulator services.
- Despite predating the formation of DHS and agency officials' acknowledgement of technological advances, the market research for a $627,000 DHS contract for satellite airtime needed to receive global

positioning data from tracking devices included in CBP aircraft had not been updated since 1999. According to agency officials, the satellite airtime was tied to the use of those particular tracking devices. Agency officials indicated they reviewed the procurement's acquisition history and issued a notice of intent to sole-source, though the notice was issued after the agency had already awarded the contract. Since the government was required to use the same vendor for both the airtime and the tracking devices, contracting officials deemed a vendor who responded to the notice ineligible. Contracting officials we spoke with acknowledged that the market research was limited and more needed to be done to assess whether there were viable alternatives to the tracking devices and its proprietary satellite airtime.

In two cases, while a lack of technical data rights may have contributed, in part, to challenges competing a contract, we nevertheless found limitations in the market research conducted to inform the acquisition approach.[31] For example:

- In a $589,000, sole-source DLA contract for actuators, the market research consisted of a presolicitation notice that was issued 2 months before the contract was signed, an examination of prior acquisition history with the incumbent, and a market survey, which was sent only to the incumbent, who did not fill it out. Although contracting officials told us that the solicitation was published on DLA's site for contracting opportunities, they also stated that there were few options for conducting market research because the product was designed to adhere to specific government requirements. In addition, officials stated that they typically rely on a program office to provide information about whether a vendor is an approved source, especially in cases where the government does not own the data rights. Contracting officials also told us that this vendor had a history of non-responsiveness and they had not expected to gather any information from the market survey.
- In a $694,000 DLA contract for controller monitors, which are one part in a piece of equipment used to provide oxygen to crew members in an aircraft, DLA faced a similar challenge because it did not own the data rights. Our contract review revealed that contracting officials had identified two sources but determined that one of the two sources was

not viable because it was a reseller that would obtain the item from the manufacturer; contracting officials told us that they did not pursue this source because they thought that the vendor would likely charge a higher price after obtaining it from the manufacturer. The other main source of market research cited in the contract's justification to sole-source was issuance of a notice of intent to sole-source, where no other vendors responded.

While market research on the lower dollar value contracts we reviewed was often limited, this was not always the case, even in situations where the contract was not competed. For example, our work found that the market research on two lower dollar value, sole-source contracts included in-depth analysis of potential sources found in the market, identification of reasons why the vendor was uniquely qualified to meet the need, and the tradeoffs that would need to be considered to compete the requirement. In one procurement involving a $1.1 million Army contract for armored windows used on mine clearance vehicles, the market research assessed three vendors and analyzed tradeoffs and costs given that the government did not own the data rights for the windows currently used. Specifically, the market research explained how the contracting officer used Internet searches to identify specific vendors, listed the vendors and websites accessed, and used this information to analyze tradeoffs associated with these potential sources. The market research also referenced attempts to gauge industry interest by issuing a sources sought notice over 6 months prior to issuing an intent to sole-source notice. The analysis quantified the time and cost associated with reverse engineering the product to produce a set of government-owned data rights, which could be used to qualify new potential sources. The justification and approval also noted that an additional vendor had expressed interest in becoming a qualified source but the agency concluded that the vendor was unsuitable for the current procurement due to the significant amount of time needed to develop a data package.

Basic Market Research Elements Were Not Consistently Documented, Limiting Use for Future Procurements

Our review found that all 28 contracts included some evidence of market research, but acquisition staff did not consistently document four basic elements in the contract file—the methods used, including the timeframes when staff used them, an analysis of the capabilities of potential sources, and a conclusion based on this analysis—which GAO determined would allow those not connected with the research to understand the market research conducted.[32] Overall, 14 of the 28 contracts we reviewed included all of these elements in the market research documentation in the contract files. However, while agency guidance describes market research documentation as useful for current and future acquisition decision making, we could not find one or more of the basic elements for 14 of the 28 contract files we reviewed, with 10 of the 14 contracts being ones we categorized as lower value. Nine of these 10 contracts were awarded by DOD and DHS (see figure 4).

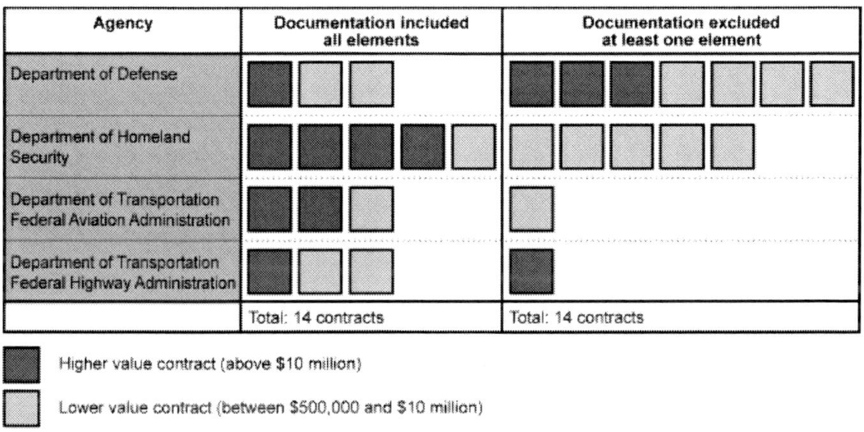

Source: GAO analysis of DOD, DHS, DOT and FAA contract documentation.| GAO-15-8.

Figure 4. Number of Contracts Whose Documentation Includes or Excludes Basic Elements.

Overall, 8 of the 12 higher dollar contracts we reviewed contained each of the basic elements, including information on potential vendors and analyses of their capabilities, information more typically missing from the lower dollar value contracts.[33] This was true whether the information was contained in an acquisition plan, the justification for other than full and open competition, or the market research report. For example, for the Army's $28.5 million contract for the procurement of advisory and assistance services, the written acquisition plan included the names of potential small business vendors who responded to the survey and an assessment of their capabilities. In another example, for an FAA procurement of a $126.6 million engine generator set program, the market research memo recorded the names of each vendor who responded to a market survey and an evaluation of their capabilities, including whether the vendor had the capacity to meet the requirement with in-house resources.

The market research documentation on the lower dollar contracts was more likely to be missing at least one element, particularly at DOD and DHS, where only 3 of the 12 lower dollar contracts we reviewed included documentation of all four elements. In particular, lower dollar value contracts were less likely to include information on potential vendors and an assessment of their capabilities. For example, the justification for other than full and open competition on CBP's $609,000 sole-source procurement for portable receiver devices awarded in September 2012 lacked information describing the capabilities of other possible vendors and the dates on which any market research was conducted. The contract specialist explained that the release of funding late in the fiscal year sometimes prevents staff from drawing up more complete market research documentation. In another example, the acquisition plan for a $2.3 million DLA contract for the lease of office copy machines lacked information about the capabilities of specific vendors. While the acquisition plan concluded that "at least five vendors could supply the equipment and associated services," it did so without identifying the market research techniques used or the names of the potential vendors. In response to our questions, the contracting office was aware of the names of the five vendors, explaining that prior information and expertise were relied upon due to the non-complexity of the requirement.

Not fully documenting basic elements of market research limits the information and insights that can be carried forward for use with subsequent contracts, especially given the potential for staff turnover in the acquisition workforce and the possibility that the need for the requirements will recur. For example, contracting and/or program staff for 5 of the 20 selected contracts we reviewed at DOD and DHS advised us that the original program or contracting staff were no longer available to respond to questions, and in two of these cases current staff could not fully respond to our questions. As we previously concluded, documenting information is particularly important given the frequent turnover in the acquisition workforce.[34] Further, according to agency officials, over three-quarters of the 20 contracts we selected at DOD and DHS provide for requirements that are likely to recur in the future, and therefore, adequately documented market research could prove useful in the future.

As we noted earlier, requiring that these basic elements be documented in contract files would be consistent with internal control standards that transactions and other significant events need to be clearly documented and the documentation should be readily available for examination so as to ensure that management directives are carried out.[35]

Market Research Helped Inform Price Reasonableness Determinations in Most of the Contracts Reviewed

The FAR identifies several techniques that can be used to help determine that a price is fair and reasonable, including a comparison between proposed prices received in response to a solicitation or a comparison between proposed prices and the independent government cost estimate.[36] While not required by the FAR or agency guidance, agencies' guidance recognizes the usefulness of market research in assessing what price would be reasonable for the government to pay for a procurement. In addition, OMB has stated that outreach to vendors is important so that the government has a clear understanding of the market place and can award a contract for an effective solution at a reasonable price.[37] Contracting officers cited one or more market research techniques as contributing to their determination of a fair and reasonable price in 21 of the 28 contracts we reviewed. The market research for 5 of these contracts involved communication with industry.

We identified the use of a variety of market research techniques in determining price reasonableness such as a review of published price lists, reviewing historical prices, and techniques involving communication with industry. While using market research to help inform the price reasonableness determination tended not to involve communication with industry, 5 contracts we reviewed did cite market research techniques that involved communication with industry. The techniques involving communication with industry included obtaining prices through requests for information posted on FedBizOpps, vendor quotes, and government requests. Two of the five were higher dollar contracts—one was competed and received multiple offers and the other was sole-sourced—where the contracting officer used pricing information received from industry in response to government requests for information to determine price reasonableness. For two of the three lower dollar contracts, the market research technique used was to obtain quotes from other vendors to compare to the proposal received—both of these were competed contracts where only one offer was received.

In 5 of the 21 cases where contracting officers cited ways that market research helped in the determination of fair and reasonable prices, contracting officers also cited how this pricing information helped the government to negotiate a price lower than what was originally proposed by the vendor. For example, in the $210 million DLA contract to provide fuel in Italy, based on our review of contract documentation, the contracting officer reviewed pricing information from the country's marketplace through published pricelists and prior contract prices, and used this information to set pricing goals for negotiations with the vendor. According to the contract file documentation, the government was able to negotiate a lower price for certain types of fuel than what the contractor had originally proposed even though only one offer was received. As we noted previously, however, DLA did not assess whether its requirement to use a printed coupon system could be modified to consider the use of a credit card system, which may have enabled DLA to obtain the benefits of market forces to help negotiate even lower prices.

In contrast, in one case in which the contracting officer cited market research as supporting a fair and reasonable price determination, we found that opportunities to use additional market research or other price reasonableness techniques may have been missed. For a 3-year, $1.5 million sole-source contract awarded by DHS for membership services to an organization that oversees the creation and use of business guidelines, agency officials were unable to provide documentation based on market research or other techniques to fully support their price reasonableness decision. The justification and approval stated that the contracting officer had determined the anticipated prices to be fair and reasonable based on price comparisons to the prior contract, and by comparing a published price list against the government's independent government cost estimate. However, DHS officials admitted that the scope of work for the previous contract was different from the scope of work for the current contract and that the contracts could not be fully compared. In addition, we found that the price of annual membership services under the current contract and as cited in its independent government cost estimate was more than 10 times higher than the price for full membership services as listed on the published price list.[38] Subsequently, a program official provided us with a high level breakdown of the costs that had been provided to the program office by the vendor prior to contract award but advised us that they had no additional documentation to support the price reasonableness determination within the program office.

For the 7 contracts that did not use market research techniques to determine price reasonableness, the contracting officers indicated that they used techniques such as comparing proposed prices to the independent government cost estimate and comparing prices among proposals received. For example, most of the competitive contracts we reviewed that received multiple offers cited the comparison of offers received as contributing to their determination of a fair and reasonable price. In addition, a contracting officer is required to obtain certified cost or pricing data from the contractor in certain instances, including for negotiated contracts above $700,000, unless an exception applies, such as obtaining adequate price competition or acquisitions of a commercial item. [39] Nearly all of the noncompeted contracts we reviewed were either below the $700,000 threshold for which certified cost or pricing data may be required, or were for commercial items, and therefore did not obtain certified cost and pricing data. In the two cases in which contracting officers were required to obtain certified cost and pricing data, we found acquisition officials did so.

CONCLUSION

Federal regulations and the agency guidance we reviewed highlighted the need to conduct and document market research commensurate with the proposed acquisitions' dollar value and complexity. We found evidence of market research in all 28 contracts we reviewed. Similarly, we often found that acquisition officials conducted more robust market research on higher dollar value contracts in particular by communicating with industry about their requirements and needs, such as through the use of requests for information. In turn, this market research appeared to contribute to higher degrees of competition for higher value contracts. Our findings also suggest, however, that agencies may be missing opportunities to promote competition and inform future acquisitions for lower dollar acquisitions. In this regard, we found DOD and DHS acquisition officials often relied on internal sources of information or simply notified potential vendors that they intended to award contracts on a sole-source basis rather than gauging whether the marketplace could offer an alternative, competitive solution. Even in situations where the government anticipates a sole-source award, market research is a tool that is required to be used to promote competition to the maximum extent practicable, and agencies generally must identify actions, if any, they may take to remove or overcome barriers to competition for future acquisitions of the supplies or services required. We also found instances in which the market research appeared to be incomplete or outdated.

Further, we found that acquisition officials omitted one or more of four basic elements of market research which GAO identified as necessary to enable others to understand the research—the methods used, the timeframes when it was conducted, an analysis of vendor capabilities, and a conclusion based on this analysis—in 14 of the 28 contracts we reviewed. These documentation shortfalls were more often, though not exclusively, found in lower value contracts. Despite DOD and DHS having guidance that either requires or recommends that specific elements be documented, contracts from these agencies accounted for all but one of the 10 lower value contracts missing one or more of the elements. While DOT documented these four elements in most of the contract files we reviewed, DOT's market research guidance does not address whether these four basic elements should be documented. As a result, DOT is at increased risk that it will not document the basic information needed to help inform current and future procurements. Federal internal control standards state that transactions and other significant events need to be clearly documented and the documentation should be readily available for examination, so as to ensure management directives are carried out. Moreover, given the recurring nature of the government's requirements covered in the contracts we reviewed and the staff turnover we observed during the course of our work, not clearly documenting such fundamental information hinders the use of market research to inform future acquisitions.

RECOMMENDATIONS FOR EXECUTIVE ACTION

To help ensure that key market research information is available for current and future use, we recommend that the Secretary of Transportation update its market research guidance to specify, at a minimum, that four basic elements—the market research methods used, the timeframes when staff used them, an analysis of the capabilities of potential sources, and a conclusion based on this analysis—be documented.

To help promote competition, inform future acquisitions, and encourage the use of timely and complete market research, we recommend that the Secretaries of Defense and Homeland Security take action to ensure their acquisition personnel clearly document the basic elements of the market research that was conducted. More specifically, documentation should, at a minimum, include the market research methods used, the timeframes when staff used them, an analysis of the capabilities of potential sources, and a conclusion based on this analysis.

AGENCY COMMENTS AND OUR EVALUATION

We provided a draft of this report to DOD, DHS, and DOT for comment. All three agencies concurred with our recommendations. The agencies' comments are summarized below. DHS and DOT provided technical comments which we incorporated into the report as appropriate.

DOD agreed with the recommendation that it take action to ensure its acquisition personnel clearly document the basic elements of market research conducted, but did not identify specific actions it intends to take. DOD noted that it recently issued a memorandum highlighting the need for effective market research to increase competition.[40] For example, the memorandum notes that contracting officers will be required to use requests for information or sources sought notices for certain procurements where a non-competitive contract is contemplated.

DHS also agreed with the recommendation that it take action to ensure its acquisition personnel clearly document the basic elements of market research conducted. DHS stated that its Office of the Chief Procurement Officer will update procedures in the Homeland Security Acquisition Manual and its market research guide to clarify that market research reports should include, at a minimum, the four basic elements. Given that we found that several DHS contract files we reviewed did not include documentation of elements already required by DHS, it will be important for DHS to ensure its contracting personnel follow its guidance.

DOT agreed with our recommendation that it update its market research guidance to identify documentation of the four basic elements, but did not elaborate on specific actions it intends to take. DOT stated that it recognizes the important role market research plays in developing sound acquisition strategies, promoting competition, and informing price reasonableness. DOT noted that its market research guidance is consistent with the requirements of the FAR, and noted that the agency continues to seek opportunities and incorporate best practices to further strengthen departmental guidance. Given the importance of written guidance in helping to ensure that management directives are implemented, we continue to encourage DOT to update its guidance to require documentation of the four basic elements on a timely basis.

Timothy J. DiNapoli,
Director
Acquisition and Sourcing Management

APPENDIX I: OBJECTIVES, SCOPE, AND METHODOLOGY

Our objectives were to assess (1) selected agencies' guidance and policy on market research and (2) how selected agencies conducted market research on selected procurements. Market research serves several purposes, including identifying sources capable of meeting the need, promoting competition, identifying whether commercial items can meet the government's needs, and identifying whether small businesses are capable of meeting the requirement. For the purposes of our review, we focused our work on how market research informed the competition strategy and the contracting officer's analysis of price reasonableness. We did not assess how market research informed the small business determination or how it informed the commerciality decision given GAO has a prior body of work that focuses on these issues.[1]

To assess agency guidance and policy on market research, we reviewed government-wide regulations and policy, such as the Federal Acquisition Regulation (FAR), including FAR Subpart 7.1—Acquisition Plans and FAR Part 10—Market Research, and Office of Management and Budget (OMB) memorandums related to market research, such as OMB's Office of Federal Procurement Policy's memorandum entitled, "Myth-Busting": Addressing Misconceptions to Improve Communication with Industry During the Acquisition Process. To assess specific agency guidance and policy and to illustrate how market research is performed at agencies of various sizes and that procure a range of products and services, we selected three departments for our review—the Departments of Defense (DOD), Homeland Security (DHS) and Transportation (DOT). We selected these departments based on their level of fiscal year 2012 contract obligations—the most recent fiscal year of information available when we started our review—and on the mix of products and services procured. Within each department, we selected two components for further review—DOD's Department of the Army and Defense Logistics Agency (DLA); DHS's Office of Procurement Operations (OPO)[2] and U.S. Customs and Border Protection (CBP); and DOT's Federal Aviation Administration (FAA) and Federal Highway Administration (FHWA). In general, we selected the components with the largest fiscal year 2012 obligations based on the Federal Procurement Data System—Next Generation (FPDS-NG). For each department and component, as applicable, we reviewed guidance and policy related to market research, including agency supplements to the FAR, market research guides and templates, acquisition handbooks, and policy memorandums that reference market research, such as DOD's Better Buying Power policy memorandums. Key agency guidance reviewed included

DOD's Defense Standardization Program, Market Research: Gathering Information about Commercial Products and Services, SD-5; DHS's Market Research Guide; DOT's Market Research Guide, Acquisition Policy DOT Dash 2010-11; and FAA's Procurement Guidance T3.2.1.2 - Market Analysis.[3] The FAR and DOT acquisition regulation do not apply to FAA acquisitions so we analyzed FAA's policy and guidance separately from DOT.[4] We did not include agency training materials as guidance for the purposes of our analyses. Further, we interviewed senior acquisition officials at each department to develop a better understanding of agency policies, guidance, and initiatives related to market research.

To assess how agencies conducted market research on selected procurements, we selected and reviewed a nongeneralizable sample of 28 contracts. For each contract, we reviewed contract documents related to market research, including market research reports, acquisition plans, justifications and approvals for sole-source awards, price negotiation memorandums and independent government cost estimates. We analyzed these documents to identify market research methods, analysis, and results used to inform the competition strategy and to inform the price reasonableness determination. To identify information that may not have been included or been self-explanatory based on our review of the contract files, we obtained additional information from agency officials. Our inquiries largely focused on identifying market research techniques that agency officials may have used but were not reflected in the contract file, as well as obtaining further explanations of any analyses they may have performed. We also analyzed contract documentation to determine whether these documents included four basic elements we identified based on our review of agency policy and guidance, which, if recorded, would allow those not connected with the market research to obtain at least a basic understanding of how the acquisition team collected and analyzed information about market capabilities. We also identified these elements because they focused on collection and analysis of information, consistent with the FAR's definition of market research.[5] The four elements included the market research methods used, including the timeframes when acquisition staff used them, an analysis of the capabilities of potential sources, and a conclusion based on this analysis.

To identify contracts for our review, we used FPDS-NG to select a nongeneralizable sample of 30 contracts awarded in fiscal year 2012 from the six components within DOD, DHS, and DOT. As our review did not focus on how market research informed the small business set-aside determination or the commercial item determination, we excluded contracts set aside for small businesses and contracts for research, development, test, and evaluation. To increase the comparability of contracts across agencies, we excluded weapons systems contracts, as they are unique to DOD. We also excluded contracts with no fiscal year 2012 obligations and contracts valued at less than $500,000, selecting this threshold as the contracts above this threshold represented more than 92 percent of contract dollars awarded in fiscal year 2012 at each component reviewed.

Within each selected agency component, we created randomized lists of the remaining fiscal year 2012 contracts within two strata—(1) contracts valued at more than $10 million and (2) contracts valued between $500,000 and $10 million. We selected two contracts from the first stratum and three from the second stratum (five per component) from the randomized lists for each component. Whereas the higher dollar stratum represented the greatest portion of contract dollars awarded in fiscal year 2012 within each component—ranging between 79 percent and 98 percent of dollars—the lower dollar stratum represented a larger portion of contract actions awarded that year. Within each stratum, we selected the contracts starting from the top of the randomized lists but applying criteria to ensure, to the extent possible, that our selected contracts within each component included at least one contract for products and one for services, at least one competed and one noncompeted contract, at least one competed contract receiving one offer and one competed contract receiving multiple offers, among other factors.

To assess the reliability of the FPDS-NG data used to select the contracts for review, we compared key data elements from FPDS-NG to the contract documentation, including contract number, agency name, and whether or not the contract had been competed using full and open competition. Where we found discrepancies relevant to our methodology, we made adjustments to maintain the integrity of our selection criteria. For example, we excluded 7 contracts because the contracts were miscoded in FPDS-NG and therefore should have been excluded from our sample. Specifically, we excluded 5 contracts because they were small business set asides, one contract because the total dollar value fell below the $500,000 threshold for inclusion in the review, and one contract because it was a research and development contract. Because we had randomized lists of contracts for each of the components, we replaced the miscoded contracts with another contract. Once we corrected for these errors, we concluded the data obtained from the FPDS-NG was sufficiently reliable for the purposes of this review.

We excluded 2 of the 30 selected contracts from our final analysis—one from FHWA and one from FAA—because, as of July 31, 2014, we were unable to assess the market research for those contracts due to missing market research documentation and staff changes since the award of the contracts.[6] As a result, our analysis in this report is based on 28 selected contracts (see table 2). The findings from our selected contracts are not generalizable to the population of all contracts within the selected agencies or components.

Table 2. Description of 28 Selected Contracts Reviewed by GAO

Contract description	Agency/ Component	Competition	Contract dollar value
Higher Dollar Contracts (above $10 million)			
Data communication integrated services	DOT/FAA	Competed, multiple offers received	$2,208,000,000
Tax-free fuel	DOD/DLA	Competed, one offer received	$210,384,000
Jet fuel with additives	DOD/DLA	Competed, multiple offers received	$157,272,000
Engine generator set program	DOT/FAA	Competed, one offer received	$126,587,000
Protective service officer services	DHS/OPO	Competed, multiple offers received	$86,993,000
Protective service officer services	DHS/OPO	Competed, multiple offers received	$76,975,000
Equipment maintenance program support and training support (bridge contract)	DHS/CBP	Noncompeted	$72,419,000
Coastal interceptor vessel	DHS/CBP	Competed, multiple offers received	$45,719,000
Advisory and assistance services	DOD/Army	Competed, multiple offers received	$28,500,000
Construction services	DOT/FHWA	Competed, multiple offers received	$23,360,000
Legal advisory services	DOT/FHWA	Competed, multiple offers received	$20,234,000
Construction services for foreign aid projects	DOD/Army	Competed, multiple offers received	$15,000,000
Lower Dollar Contracts (between $500,000 and $10 million)			
Technical and program support	DOT/FHWA	Competed, multiple offers received	$9,642,000
Transportation standards development support	DOT/FHWA	Noncompeted	$7,479,000

Table 2. (Continued)

Contract description	Agency/ Component	Competition	Contract dollar value
Construction of utilities infrastructure	DOD/Army	Noncompeted	$4,047,000
Lease of copiers, multifunction devices	DOD/DLA	Competed, multiple offers received	$2,259,000
Flight simulator training	DOD/Army	Competed, one offer received	$2,067,000
Relocation of Doppler navigation system	DOT/FAA	Competed, multiple offers received	$1,631,000
Parking	DHS/OPO	Competed, one offer received	$1,585,000
Standards organization membership services	DHS/OPO	Noncompeted	$1,500,000
Armor, transparent, vehicular window	DOD/Army	Noncompeted	$1,132,000
Recycle and store tubes of helium	DHS/OPO	Noncompeted	$983,000
Jail space services	DHS/CBP	Competed, one offer received	$846,000
Controller monitors	DOD/DLA	Noncompeted	$694,000
Satellite airtime	DHS/CBP	Noncompeted	$627,000
Portable receiver systems	DHS/CBP	Noncompeted	$609,000
Actuators	DOD/DLA	Noncompeted	$589,000
Furniture, workstations	DOT/FAA	Noncompeted	$538,000

Source: GAO analysis of agency documentation. | GAO-15-8.

We conducted this performance audit from August 2013 to October 2014 in accordance with generally accepted government auditing standards. Those standards require that we plan and perform the audit to obtain sufficient, appropriate evidence to provide a reasonable basis for our findings and conclusions based on our audit objectives. We believe that the evidence obtained provides a reasonable basis for our findings and conclusions based on our audit objectives.

End Notes

[1] Office of Management and Budget, Office of Federal Procurement Policy, "Myth-Busting': Addressing Misconceptions to Improve Communication with Industry During the Acquisition Process, Memorandum for Chief Acquisition Officers, Senior Procurement

Representatives, Chief Information Officers (Washington, D.C.: Feb. 2, 2011) and Office of Management and Budget, Office of Federal Procurement Policy, "Myth-Busting 2': Addressing Misconceptions and Further Improving Communication During the Acquisition Process, Memorandum for Chief Acquisition Officers, Senior Procurement Representatives, Chief Information Officers (Washington, D.C.: May 7, 2012).

[2] For the purposes of this report, we considered DHS's Office of Procurement Operations to be a component.

[3] While this review focused on guidance applicable across each department and separately for FAA, FHWA noted its Acquisition Customer Service Guide contains additional information on market research techniques.

[4] For the purposes of this report, we use the term agency policy and guidance to refer to that issued by DOD, DHS, DOT, as well as FAA. The FAR does not apply to FAA acquisitions pursuant to the Department of Transportation and Related Agencies Appropriations Act of 1996, Pub. L. No. 104-50 § 348 (1995).

[5] At the conclusion of our review in August 2014, FHWA officials reported they had located the preaward documents for the contract. For the FAA contract, contracting staff were unable to locate the market research for the contract. In both instances the staff responsible for conducting, documenting, or accepting the market research were no longer with the organization.

[6] For GAO's recent work on commercial item determinations, see GAO, Federal Contracting: Commercial Item Test Program Beneficial, but Actions Needed to Mitigate Potential Risks, GAO-14-178 (Washington D.C.: Feb. 4, 2014). For GAO's recent work on small business contracting, see GAO, Small Business Contracting: Updated Guidance and Reporting Needed for Consolidated Contracts, GAO-14-36 (Washington D.C.: Nov. 26, 2013).

[7] Pub. L. No. 98-369, Div. B, tit. VII, § 2711.

[8] FAR § 10.000.

[9] FAR § 10.001(a)(2). The simplified acquisition threshold is generally $150,000.

[10] FAR § 10.002(b)(1).

[11] GAO, Acquisition Planning: Opportunities to Build Strong Foundations for Better Services Contracts, GAO-11-672 (Washington, D.C.: Aug. 9, 2011).

[12] GAO, Defense Contracting: Improved Policies and Tools Could Help Increase Competition on DOD's National Security Exception Procurements, GAO-12-263 (Washington, D.C.: Jan. 13, 2012); GAO, Defense Contracting: Actions Needed to Increase Competition, GAO-13-325 (Washington, D.C.: Mar. 28, 2013).

[13] GAO, Strategic Sourcing: Leading Commercial Practices Can Help Federal Agencies Increase Savings When Acquiring Services, GAO-13-417 (Washington, D.C.: Apr. 15, 2013).

[14] GAO, Defense Contracting: Early Attention in the Acquisition Process Needed to Enhance Competition, GAO-14-395 (Washington, D.C., May 5, 2014).

[15] GAO, Federal Contracting: Noncompetitive Contracts Based on Urgency Need Additional Oversight, GAO-14-304 (Washington, D.C.: Mar. 26, 2014).

[16] GAO, Federal Contracting: Opportunities Exist to Increase Competition and Assess Reasons When Only One Offer is Received, GAO-10-833 (Washington, D.C.: Jul. 26, 2010).

[17] FAR § 7.102(a).

[18] FAR § 7.102(a) and (b).

[19] FAR § 15.404-1(b)(2)(vi).

[20] FAR § 7.102(a)(2). The FAR also directs that the results of market research are to be used to determine if sources capable of satisfying the agency's requirements exist. FAR § 10.001(a)(3)(i).

[21] Subpart 6.3 of the FAR specifies the conditions under which an agency may award a contract to a single source without providing for full and open competition. The award of such a contract can be referred to as a sole-source award.

[22] FAR § 15.404-1(b)(2)(vi).

[23] Section 10.002(b)(2) of the FAR lists techniques for conducting market research.

[24] FAA published its vendor communication plan in July 2009, prior to the OMB initiative.

[25] See OMB, "Myth-Busting" Memorandum (Washington, D.C.: Feb. 2, 2011) and OMB, "Myth-Busting 2" Memorandum (Washington, D.C.: May 7, 2012).

[26] FAR § 7.105(b)(1). FAR § 7.103(e) directs that agency heads determine criteria and thresholds under which increasingly greater detail and formality in the planning process is required.

[27] FAR § 6.303-2(b)(8). The FAR outlines similar requirements for orders and blanket purchase agreements above the simplified acquisition threshold established under the federal supply schedules without using competitive procedures. See FAR § 8.405- 6(c)(2)(vi).

[28] DOD's template applies specifically to services acquisitions.

[29] GAO, Internal Control: Standards for Internal Control in the Federal Government, GAO/AIMD-00-21.3.1 (Washington, D.C.: November, 1999).

[30] FAR Part 5.2 generally requires agencies to publish notice on FedBizOpps of proposed contract actions.

[31] With regards to the issue of a lack of technical data rights, DLA officials noted that DLA is responsible for sustainment of weapons systems and does not have data rights for many items they procure. DLA officials stated that if potential alternate sources are not found during market research prior to issuing a solicitation, then DLA Directive clause 52.217-9002 "Conditions for Evaluation of Offers for Part Numbered Items" may be included in the solicitation. This clause may be used in negotiated acquisitions of replacement parts, components, and assemblies which are identified only by the name of the approved source, a part number, and a brief description, and the clause provides, among other things, that vendors can offer an alternate product, which could increase competition. DLA Directive § §17.7501(b)(3)(i); 52.217-9002.

[32] In the absence of guidance from DOT, we compared the contents of DOD, DHS, and FAA guidance to identify the minimum elements which, if recorded in the contract file, would allow others, such as reviewers or those procuring similar items in the future, to understand the nature of the market research conducted, potential sources, and how it was used.

[33] In response to GAO's finding that one of FHWA's higher dollar contracts did not include documentation of all four elements, FHWA officials told us that they considered the market research conducted on the $20 million contract for legal advisory services to be extensive, noting that as a part of market research the agency reached out to dozens of potential sources. The officials acknowledged, however, that better documentation of the analysis of the capabilities of these sources would have strengthened the overall market research.

[34] GAO-11-672.

[35] GAO/AIMD-00-21.3.1.

[36] The contracting officer may use an independent government cost estimate to help establish the reasonableness of contractors' costs or prices.

[37] See OMB, "Myth-Busting" Memorandum (Washington, D.C.: Feb. 2, 2011).

[38] A program official told us that the published price list reflected a basic membership price and the total contract price included the price for additional membership services outlined in the statement of work, such as access to international standards, workshops convened by a panel focused on the development and adoption of standards critical to homeland security,

and a database. However, there was no documentation to support the price reasonableness of these additional services included in the contract file.

[39] FAR §15.403-4.

[40] DOD, Office of the Under Secretary for Acquisition, Technology, and Logistics, Actions to Improve Department of Defense Competition (Washington, D.C.: Aug. 21, 2014).

End Notes for Appendix I

[1] For GAO's recent work on commercial item determinations, see GAO, Federal Contracting: Commercial Item Test Program Beneficial, but Actions Needed to Mitigate Potential Risks, GAO-14-178 (Washington D.C.: Feb. 4, 2014). For GAO's recent work on small business contracting, see GAO, Small Business Contracting: Updated Guidance and Reporting Needed for Consolidated Contracts, GAO-14-36 (Washington D.C.: Nov. 26, 2013).

[2] For the purposes of this report, we considered DHS's Office of Procurement Operations to be a component.

[3] While this review focused on guidance applicable across each department and separately for FAA, FHWA noted its Acquisition Customer Service Guide contains additional information on market research techniques.

[4] For the purposes of this report, we use the term agency policy and guidance to refer to that issued by DOD, DHS, DOT, as well as FAA. The FAR does not apply to FAA acquisitions pursuant to the Department of Transportation and Related Agencies Appropriations Act, 1996. Pub. L. No. 104-50, § 348 (1995).

[5] FAR § 2.101 defines market research as the process used to collect and analyze data about capabilities in the market that could satisfy an agency's procurement needs.

[6] At the conclusion of our review in August 2014, FHWA officials reported they had located the preaward documents for the contract. For the FAA contract, contracting staff were unable to locate the market research for the contract. In both instances the staff responsible for conducting, documenting, or accepting the market research were no longer with the organization.

In: Market Research
Editor: Cherese Hartell

ISBN: 978-1-63482-008-0

Chapter 2

"MYTH-BUSTING": ADDRESSING MISCONCEPTIONS TO IMPROVE COMMUNICATION WITH INDUSTRY DURING THE ACQUISITION PROCESS*

Daniel Gordon

With expenditures of over $500 billion annually on contracts and orders for goods and services, the federal government has an obligation to conduct our procurements in the most effective, responsible, and efficient manner possible. Access to current market information is critical for agency program managers as they define requirements and for contracting officers as they develop acquisition strategies, seek opportunities for small businesses, and negotiate contract terms. Our industry partners are often the best source of this information, so productive interactions between federal agencies and our industry partners should be encouraged to ensure that the government clearly understands the marketplace and can award a contract or order for an effective solution at a reasonable price. Early, frequent, and constructive engagement with industry is especially important for complex, high-risk procurements, including (but not limited to) those for large information technology (IT) projects. This is why increasing communication, in the form of a "myth-

* This is an edited, reformatted and augmented version of a memorandum issued by the Office of Management and Budget, Office of Federal Procurement Policy, Februrary 2, 2011.

busters" educational campaign, is one of the key tenets of the Office of Management and Budget's 25 Point Implementation Plan to Reform Federal IT Management.[1]

The Federal Acquisition Regulation (FAR) authorizes a broad range of opportunities for vendor communication[2], but agencies often do not take full advantage of these existing flexibilities. Some agency officials may be reluctant to engage in these exchanges out of fear of protests or fear of binding the agency in an unauthorized manner; others may be unaware of effective strategies that can help the acquisition workforce and industry make the best use of their time and resources. Similarly, industry may be concerned that talking with an agency may create a conflict of interest that will preclude them from competing on future requirements, or industry may be apprehensive about engaging in meaningful conversations in the presence of other vendors.

In light of these challenges, the purposes of this memorandum are to:

1) identify common misconceptions about vendor engagement that may be unnecessarily hindering agencies' appropriate use of the existing flexibilities, and provide facts and strategies to help acquisition professionals benefit from industry's knowledge and insight;
2) direct agencies to remove unnecessary barriers to reasonable communication and develop vendor communications plans, consistent with existing law and regulation, that promote responsible and constructive exchanges; and
3) outline steps for continued engagement with agencies and industry to increase awareness and education.

Nothing in this memorandum should be read to alter, or authorize violations of, applicable ethics rules, procurement integrity requirements, or other statutes or regulations that govern communication and information sharing. However, all methods of communication that are not prohibited, either by those rules or otherwise, should be considered, if they would be helpful.[3] In addition, contracting officers, program managers, and other acquisition officials should continue to exercise appropriate discretion to balance the practical limitations of frequent vendor engagement, including the demand such engagement places on the time of the acquisition workforce, with the need to better understand the market and make decisions in the best interest of the government.

Top 10 Misconceptions and Facts

The Office of Federal Procurement Policy (OFPP) held a series of outreach sessions with industry representatives, acquisition professionals, agency procurement attorneys, and others to identify and address core misconceptions about communication between the government and industry during the pre-award acquisition process. While these conversations will continue, as discussed later, ten misconceptions were mentioned frequently, and so are addressed by this memorandum. Attachment 1 lists these issues, and provides additional information and strategies to help agencies promote fair and appropriate engagement during various acquisition phases.

Vendor Communication Plan

Some agencies have developed policies for communicating with industry while others have not, resulting in disparate practices and confusion. To provide better direction to the workforce and to clarify the nature and schedule of engagement opportunities for industry, each agency should develop a high-level vendor communication plan. The plan should discuss how the agency will reduce unnecessary barriers, publicize communication opportunities, and prioritize engagement opportunities for high-risk, complex programs or those that fail to attract new vendors during re-competitions. Details on the required elements of this plan are included in Attachment 2.

The 24 Chief Financial Officer (CFO) Act agencies are required to develop a vendor communication plan; to make these plans available to their workforce and the public, as appropriate; and to update them at least annually. These agencies shall submit their draft plans, by June 30, 2011, for review by the Office of Management and Budget. The draft plans will be reviewed by the Administrator for Federal Procurement Policy and the Federal Chief Information Officer (CIO) to ensure that agencies are encouraging more communication, taking advantage of existing authorities, and educating their workforce on communication opportunities. Based on this review, the agencies will finalize their plans and make them available to their workforce and to the public, as appropriate, no later than 30 days after the completion of OMB's review. Small agencies are encouraged to review their existing vendor communication guidance in light of the principles discussed in this memorandum and make appropriate modifications to encourage more communication, or develop guidance if none exists.

Increasing Awareness

Throughout 2011, OFPP will work with the Federal Acquisition Institute (FAI), the Defense Acquisition University (DAU), and agency training practitioners to conduct an awareness campaign to eliminate unnecessary barriers to engagement. As agencies work to develop and refine their vendor communications plans, they will be supported by a number of efforts:

Continued Discussion

Expansion of the conversation between industry and government and the education on both sides must continue in an open, transparent forum. To support this discussion, agencies and industry are invited to join a moderated, online dialogue starting in mid-February to help identify additional misconceptions, concerns, perceived conflicts in policies, and success stories that will help improve communications between government and industry. Additional information on how to participate in this and other discussions will be made available on www.caoc.gov and www.cioc.gov.

Community of Practice (COP)

To help agencies increase and improve vendor engagement, OFPP and E-Gov will launch an online COP no later than June 2011 that will provide additional strategies, do's and don'ts for agencies and for vendors, frequently asked questions, agency and industry success stories, case studies, and other tools to improve engagement. Next month, OFPP will convene a working group of federal acquisition professionals to help define the requirements of this site. If you are interested in participating in this working group, please identify your agency's point of contact by February 14 to Mindy Connolly of OFPP at mconnolly@omb.eop.gov.

Training and Outreach

FAI will develop a continuous learning module that contracting officers, program managers, procurement attorneys, and others can utilize to develop a better understanding of the types of permissible communication. This is scheduled to be available early in the third quarter of FY 2011 on the FAI website – www.fai.gov. Additionally, FAI and OFPP will provide sessions at widely-attended procurement conferences throughout 2011 to increase awareness of the need for more industry engagement. Agencies should provide similar training or outreach efforts, especially to their front line acquisition and program personnel.

Acquisition Communication Platform

In accordance with the 25 Point Implementation Plan to Reform Federal IT Management, the General Services Administration is seeking input from agencies, industry, and other stakeholders on developing a communication platform that would facilitate exchanges for specific planned acquisitions. This platform will allow the government to more easily engage the vendor community during the pre-solicitation stage, and may be further developed to facilitate communication during other stages of the acquisition. Development of the requirements will consider existing platforms and functionality and will be developed in collaboration with the Integrated Acquisition Environment. Additional details will be communicated to the community as they become available.

Conclusion

While agencies do not have the resources, and are not required, to meet with every vendor at every step of the acquisition process, information gathered from industry sources plays an invaluable role in the acquisition process. For this reason, agencies must develop practices that will ensure early, frequent, and constructive communication during key phases of the process. The federal government's ability to achieve successful program outcomes, effectively and efficiently, depends upon agencies establishing effective strategies for industry engagement and supporting those strategies with senior-level commitment.

Thank you for your commitment to this important matter. Please contact Mindy Connolly on (202) 395-7724 or mconnolly@omb.eop.gov if you have any questions.

Attachments

Attachment 1 –Misconceptions and Facts about Vendor Communication
Attachment 2 - Vendor Communication Plans
cc:
Agency General Counsels and Solicitors
Agency Ethics Officers

ATTACHMENT 1. MISCONCEPTIONS AND FACTS ABOUT VENDOR COMMUNICATION

1.	Misconception – "We can't meet one-on-one with a potential offeror."
	Fact – Government officials can generally meet one-on-one with potential offerors as long as no vendor receives preferential treatment.

Prior to issuance of the solicitation, government officials – including the program manager, users, or contracting officer – may meet with potential offerors to exchange general information and conduct market research related to an acquisition. In fact, the FAR, in Part 15, encourages exchanges of information with interested parties during the solicitation process, ending with the receipt of proposals. There is no requirement that the meetings include all possible offerors, nor is there a prohibition on one-on-one meetings. Any information that is shared in a meeting that could directly affect proposal preparation must be shared in a timely manner with *all* potential offerors to avoid providing any offeror with an unfair advantage (FAR 15.201(f)).

The government ethics rules and Competition in Contracting Act, (10 U.S.C. § 2304), prohibit preferential treatment of one vendor over another. Where vendor interaction is expected to include contract terms and conditions, any one-on-one meetings should include, or at least be coordinated with, the contracting officer (FAR 15.201).[4] After the solicitation is issued, the contracting officer shall be the focal point for these exchanges. (Special rules govern communications with offerors after receipt of proposals; that situation is not addressed here.)

Some vendors have expressed concern that involvement in pre-solicitation discussions might lead to exclusion resulting from organizational conflict of interest (OCI) concerns. This should not be the case. While a vendor who, as part of contract performance, drafts the specification for a future procurement will almost certainly be barred by OCI rules from competing for that future procurement, pre-solicitation communications are generally less structured, less binding, and much less problematic. When a vendor, in its role supporting the government, is drafting specifications for a future acquisition, the government is relying on the vendor to provide impartial advice regarding the requirements needed to meet the government's future needs. Ensuring that the vendor will not be motivated by a desire to win the future contract is the way we try to ensure that this advice will be impartial. This differs dramatically from the pre-solicitation context. In the latter context, the government is not looking for impartial advice from one source, but is instead looking for a variety of options from a variety of sources, each one understandably, and reasonably, attempting to demonstrate the value of its own approach. These marketing efforts, in themselves, do not raise OCI concerns.

2.	Misconception – "Since communication with contractors is like communication with registered lobbyists, and since contact with lobbyists must be disclosed, additional communication with contractors will involve a substantial additional disclosure burden, so we should avoid these meetings."
	Fact – Disclosure is required only in certain circumstances, such as for meetings with registered lobbyists. Many contractors do not fall into this category, and even when disclosure is required, it is normally a minimal burden that should not prevent a useful meeting from taking place.

Disclosure is an important tool that ensures public trust in our contracting process, but it should not be an impediment to meeting with contractors and is not required in every circumstance. In the case of meetings where registered lobbyists are employed, contractors are required to track the costs and activities of their lobbying activities, as required by FAR Part 31, but that obligation places the disclosure burden on the contractor and does not require the government to take any steps. In this "standard" case, additional communication with contractors will not involve an additional disclosure burden, though conduct of all communications should be consistent with the principles of fairness and accountability. Moreover, this rule only applies in those circumstances where a contractor or one or more of its employees are registered lobbyists, which will not be the case in every meeting.

There have been additional requirements for disclosure regarding spending under the American Recovery and Reinvestment Act (ARRA). Government officials are required by the March 2009 Presidential memorandum on "Ensuring Responsible Spending of Recovery Act Funds"[5] to disclose discussions with registered lobbyists related to ARRA procurements. Any ARRA procurement that was conducted with involvement from registered lobbyists does carry this additional disclosure requirement (only a small number of all procurements during this period were obligated using funding from ARRA).

Another source of concern might be the additional ethical commitments required of political appointees by Executive Order 13490, "Ethics Commitments by Executive Branch Personnel." While the ethics pledge required by this Executive Order does extend and strengthen certain limitations on actions by government personnel, most notably with respect to pre- and post-employment restrictions, the pledge does not create general barriers to meeting with industry to discuss procurements. The pledge prohibits some contact with former clients and former employers for two years, which might create a specific limitation in some circumstances, but it does not establish a general prohibition on meeting with registered lobbyists, even in one-on-one circumstances.

Finally, even in the special situations where disclosure is required, that should not be a reason for avoiding communication in situations where the communication will improve the procurement and provide better value to the taxpayer.

<table>
<tr><td rowspan="2">3</td><td>Misconception – "A protest is something to be avoided at all costs - even if it means the government limits conversations with industry."</td></tr>
<tr><td>Fact – Restricting communication won't prevent a protest, and limiting communication might actually increase the chance of a protest – in addition to depriving the government of potentially useful information.</td></tr>
</table>

Protests are, in fact, quite rare. At least 99 percent of procurements are never protested, although high dollar procurements, of course, are more likely to be protested. The overriding goal of the agency and its program managers, contracting officers, and attorneys should be the best procurement solution, and industry engagement can improve the supplies or services received or can reduce the price paid by the government. If contracting officers conduct responsible, meaningful, and constructive communications during the course of a procurement, issues that could give rise to a bid protest are likely eliminated. Trying to make a procurement 'protest-proof' is rarely a good use of agency resources, and it may lead to decisions that aren't in the interest of the government. Moreover, restricting communication for fear of protests may actually increase the likelihood of a protest – for example, by a vendor that hopes to get more information through 'discovery' during the protest.

4.	Misconception – "Conducting discussions/negotiations after receipt of proposals will add too much time to the schedule."
	Fact – Whether discussions should be conducted is a key decision for contracting officers to make. Avoiding discussions solely because of schedule concerns may be counter-productive, and may cause delays and other problems during contract performance.

Although the government often states it intends to award without discussions/negotiations, the clause at FAR 52.215-1[6] reserves the government's option to conduct discussions and it is usually a good practice to retain that option.

While discussions may add time to the acquisition schedule, the contracting officer should make a thoughtful decision as to whether to conduct discussions and, if so, what the scope and extent of discussions required should be. Schedule pressures should generally not be the primary, or even a strong, driver in the contracting officer's decision on whether or not to hold discussions. One consideration the contracting officer should take into account is that conducting robust pre-solicitation communications with industry may actually minimize the need for discussions and result in a better technical solution and improved contract performance. Other considerations include the complexity of the procurement, and the history of change orders on previous or related contracts that were due to lack of a clear understanding of the requirements and contract terms and conditions by the parties. In situations where discussions are not held, post-award contract modifications that increase the government's costs are often required. These costly changes are negotiated after the government has lost the benefits of a competitive environment.

When discussions are considered helpful to obtaining the best outcome in a procurement, the schedule should be developed accordingly. Contracting officers should be empowered by their management to make these judgment calls on a case-by-case basis and should have the full support of their customers.

5.	Misconception – "If the government meets with vendors, that may cause them to submit an unsolicited proposal and that will delay the procurement process."
	Fact – Submission of an unsolicited proposal should not affect the schedule. Generally, the unsolicited proposal process is separate from the process for a known agency requirement that can be acquired using competitive methods.

All acquisition officials should be familiar with FAR Subpart 15.6 and their agency's procedures for receiving and evaluating an unsolicited proposal. Receipt of unsolicited proposals should not cause delay in an acquisition.

6.	Misconception – "When the government awards a task or delivery order using the Federal Supply Schedules, debriefing the offerors isn't required so it shouldn't be done."
	Fact – Providing feedback is important, both for offerors and the government, so agencies should generally provide feedback whenever possible.

Although debriefings are not required when using the Federal Supply Schedules (FSS) under FAR Part 8.4 procedures, even in those situations, agencies are instructed to "provide a brief explanation of the basis for the award decision" where the award was based upon factors other than price (FAR 8.405-2(d)). Agencies that order from FSS contracts regularly are missing an important feedback opportunity if they do not take time to explain to FSS offerors how to improve their offers in the future. For newer contracting officers, the less structured explanation required for FSS offerors can be a valuable learning opportunity to prepare for structured debriefings. In both FSS and FAR Part 15 procurements, agencies are encouraged to provide the maximum amount of relevant information to offerors, rather than focusing on sharing only the minimum that is legally required.

7 .	Misconception – "Industry days and similar events attended by multiple vendors are of low value to industry and the government because industry won't provide useful information in front of competitors, and the government doesn't release new information."

	Fact – Well-organized industry days, as well as pre-solicitation and pre-proposal conferences, are valuable opportunities for the government and for potential vendors – both prime contractors and subcontractors, many of whom are small businesses.

Industry days, as well as pre-solicitation and pre-proposal conferences, directly benefit the government by promoting a common understanding of the procurement requirements, the solicitation terms and conditions, and the evaluation criteria. These events also benefit industry – especially small businesses – by providing prime contractors and subcontractors an opportunity to meet and develop relationships or teaming agreements that benefit contract performance. However, the value of these events derives from the government providing the maximum information to potential offerors on its requirements, answering questions, and improving the solicitation based on feedback from the potential offerors. In that way, the requirements can be made as clear as possible to assist potential offerors in providing the best solution to the government.

Strategy - where appropriate, use interactive web-based technology to expand the reach of the exchange, such as a live webinar with streaming video to immediately address questions from stakeholders. Consider combining this with immediate one-on-one meetings with vendors to make these engagements more useful, especially for large, complex requirements.

8.	Misconception – "The program manager already talked to industry to develop the technical requirements, so the contracting officer doesn't need to do anything else before issuing the RFP."
	Fact – The technical requirements are only part of the acquisition; getting feedback on terms and conditions, pricing structure, performance metrics, evaluation criteria, and contract administration matters will improve the award and implementation process.

Issuing a high quality solicitation requires engaging with industry on issues that go beyond the government's technical requirements. In order to appropriately price proposals and reduce the number of potential change orders, industry needs information about any unique terms and conditions, small business set-aside requirements, subcontracting goals, and other matters about which the contracting officer is the expert. Although industry may have had their best technical representatives engaged with the program manager, the contracting officer should communicate to vendors as much information as possible about the government's needs as early as possible. As a result of early communication, the contracting officer may learn some things that suggest that an approach somewhat different than planned may cause increased competition, more small business participation, lower prices, or even a better definition of the government's technical requirements.

Strategy – Issue an RFI to make sure the government not only understands the capabilities of industry, but can develop or improve its acquisition strategy regarding contract type, performance requirements, performance work statements/statements of work, and performance metrics. Release a draft request for proposal, including sections L and M, to be sure the solicitation instructions are clear.

9.	Misconception – "Giving industry only a few days to respond to an RFP is OK since the government has been talking to industry about this procurement for over a year."
	Fact – Providing only short response times may result in the government receiving fewer proposals and the ones received may not be as well-developed - which can lead to a flawed contract. This approach signals that the government isn't really interested in competition.

While the FAR does contain some requirements on the length of time between issuance of solicitations and proposal due dates, often task and delivery orders do not have these requirements. Contracting officers should consider that allowing offerors additional time to prepare their proposals will likely yield better proposals, streamlined evaluations, and a reduction in the need for (or scope of) discussions. While the workforce is stretched thin and requirements often arise unexpectedly, shortcutting the proposal development process often results in fewer proposals, and/or proposals that are more difficult to evaluate. This situation can lead to expensive outcomes. Providing adequate time for vendor communication throughout the procurement process – including adequate time for proposals – indicates that the government is interested in obtaining the best outcomes. Contracting officers should have the full support of their customers in determining the right amount of time for receipt of proposals.

10.	Misconception – "Getting broad participation by many different vendors is too difficult; we're better off dealing with the established companies we know."

	Fact – The government loses when we limit ourselves to the companies we already work with. Instead, we need to look for opportunities to increase competition and ensure that all vendors, including small businesses, get fair consideration.

FAR Section 10.002 expressly allows for participation in interactive, online communications among industry, acquisition personnel, and customers. While agencies should ensure that these tools can be used securely and appropriately, their use should be encouraged to the maximum extent practicable. In accordance with OMB's 25 Point Implementation Plan to Reform Federal IT Management, GSA and OMB will be developing an acquisition communications platform for launch in June 2011 that will increase collaboration on RFIs and draft RFPs, improve communication during question and answer periods, and otherwise support better engagement. Agencies may also have similar tools, and their use should be encouraged.

Strategy – Use the procurement forecast to generate interest and publicize those opportunities available to small businesses. Ensure that the points of contact on the forecast are aware of the content and timing of the release of the document so they can address any inquiries, consider holding an outreach session or webinar to announce the release or update, and don't bundle or overpromise requirements. Hold industry days, public meetings, or small business conferences, and consider hosting multiple outreach sessions for large or complex requirements.

ATTACHMENT 2. VENDOR COMMUNICATION PLANS

Agencies should provide clear, consistent direction to their workforce and industry partners about how to engage with industry prior to the award of contracts and task and delivery orders under the Federal Supply Schedule, government-wide acquisition contracts, and other indefinite delivery/indefinite quantity contracts.

To ensure this, agencies shall develop high-level plans that include the core elements listed below. These plans should be general in nature and can build on existing guidance. OFPP will work with the agencies in the development of the community of practice discussed earlier to identify best practices, training opportunities, samples of guidance, and other information that may be helpful in developing these communication plans.

1) Statement of agency commitment to:
   a) Communicate early, frequently, and constructively with industry;
   b) Include small businesses and subgroups of small businesses in communications with industry;
   c) Include vendors that the agency has not worked with in the past;
   d) Identify, in the agency's published procurement forecast, which procurements are likely to involve opportunity for additional communication with industry; and
   e) Protect non-public information including vendors' confidential information and the agency's source selection information.
2) Identification of senior agency and bureau (if applicable) official responsible for promoting vendor engagement;
3) Brief description of efforts undertaken or planned to reduce barriers and promote engagement;
4) Criteria for identifying which acquisitions must include vendor input in the pre-award phase and the extent of the required engagement as a condition of approval by the agency's investment review board (or similar body). At a minimum, acquisition plans for high-risk, large-dollar, and complex programs, such as those for major IT systems and for re-competitions that need to attract new entrants to ensure adequate competition, should include a comprehensive vendor engagement strategy that:
   - includes at least one industry day or a pre-solicitation or pre-proposal conference; and
   - allows for a reasonable amount of one-on-one engagement; and
   - allows time for discussions, as needed and in accordance with FAR Part 15, during the proposal evaluation process; or
   - requires a written justification as to why those steps are unnecessary.
5) Publication of engagement events to include industry days, small business outreach sessions, pre-solicitation conferences, RFP question and answer sessions, etc. These shall be posted and updated regularly using the existing "special notices" function on www.fedbizopps.gov and on other sites as identified by the agency.7
6) Brief description of roles and responsibilities of the –
   a) Contracting Officer
   b) Program Manager
   c) COR/COTR
   d) General Counsel

   e) Ethics Officers
   f) OSDBU
   g) Other Officials[8]

7) Training and awareness efforts for employees and contractors;
8) Links to existing policies; and
9) Plans to follow-up with employees and industry representatives within 6 months of posting the vendor engagement plan, to further refine and improve communication, (e.g., post-award surveys of the contracting officers, program managers, and offerors for large, complex procurements, focus group meetings for general feedback).

End Notes

[1] 25 Point Implementation Plan to Reform Federal Information Technology Management available at http://cio.gov/documents/25-Point-Implementation-Plan-to-Reform-Federal%20IT.pdf

[2] For example, FAR 10.002(b)(2) authorizes a wide range of techniques for conducting market research, including participation in interactive, online communications with industry.

[3] See FAR Part 1.102(d) stating that if a specific strategy, practice, policy or procedure is in the best interests of the government and is not addressed in the FAR, nor prohibited by law (statute or case law), Executive Order or other regulation, then the strategy, practice, policy or procedure is a permissible exercise of authority.

[4] Under sealed bidding procedures, in accordance with FAR Part 14, only the contracting officer, superior, or other authorized individual can transmit this information.

[5] Available at http://www.whitehouse.gov/the_press_office/Memorandum-for-the-Heads-of-Executive-Departmentsand-Agencies-3-20-09/.

[6] When preparing solicitations, contracting officers should carefully evaluate whether to include the clause at 52.215-1 or its Alternate 1.

[7] Instructions for posting such events on www.fedbizopps.gov will be provided to agency points of contact for vendor communication as needed.

[8] Such as those identified in the procurement forecast.

In: Market Research
Editor: Cherese Hartell
ISBN: 978-1-63482-008-0

Chapter 3

"Myth-Busting 2": Addressing Misconceptions and Further Improving Communication with Industry During the Acquisition Process*

Lesley A. Field

Early, frequent, and constructive engagement with industry leads to better acquisition outcomes, which is why it is one of the key tenets of the Office of Management and Budget's 25 Point Implementation Plan to Reform Federal IT Management.[1] Such engagement is especially important for complex, high-risk procurements, including (but not limited to) those for large information technology (IT) projects.

To that end, the Office of Federal Procurement Policy (OFPP) last year issued the "Myth-Busting" memorandum on "Addressing Misconceptions to Improve Communication with Industry during the Acquisition Process."[2] In the subsequent months, Federal agencies have taken significant additional steps to improve communications between Federal agencies and the vendor community. These developments are discussed further below.

To continue to make progress in improving these communications, OFPP is issuing this second "Myth-Busting" memorandum. Whereas we focused last

---

* This is an edited, reformatted and augmented version of a memorandum issued by the Office of Management and Budget, Office of Federal Procurement Policy, May 7, 2012.

year on the misconceptions on the part of Federal agencies, we want to continue the discussion by addressing in this memorandum the misconceptions that may be held by some in the vendor community. As we did last year, we highlight the misconceptions in the Attachment and, for each one, provide the facts about the Federal procurement process, with the goal of improving the productivity of our communications. The Attachment also provides additional information and strategies for both agencies and vendors to promote more effective communication.[3]

We encourage you to share this information with current and potential industry partners – especially those new to government contracting – as part of your outreach efforts to ensure that we are collectively making the best use of our engagement opportunities.

As part of the ongoing, government-wide effort to improve vendor communication, OFPP and OMB's Office of E-Government and Information Technology worked with the Chief Financial Officers (CFO) Act agencies to develop vendor communications plans for:

- reducing barriers to communication,
- incorporating more industry input into agency acquisitions, publicizing engagement events, and
- providing training and awareness to employees and vendors.

To increase vendor awareness of these plans and upcoming engagement opportunities, the Chief Acquisition Officers Council worked with the Integrated Acquisition Environment team at the General Services Administration to add a new vendor collaboration feature on the FedBizOpps homepage (www.fbo.gov). Through this Vendor Collaboration Central Event Listing, vendors have quick and easy access to agencies' engagement opportunities, such as industry days, pre-Request for Proposal (RFP) conferences, vendor forums, etc. (Agencies are encouraged to post their upcoming events in accordance with the instructions found on FedBizOpps.)

Since the first "Myth-Busters" memorandum was issued last year, agencies have taken strong steps to promote effective strategies for engagement, including the following examples:

- The Nuclear Regulatory Commission uses several avenues for vendor outreach:
  - Quarterly Business Seminars to educate vendors about the agency,

    - One-on-one discussions between vendors and project managers regarding current technology and future requirements, and
    - Technical counseling sessions for market research on specific requirements.
- The Department of Education held a webinar with prospective offerors in the presolicitation phase of the English Language Learners Professional Development Network procurement.
    - The webinar was advertised on FedBizOpps, and 55 vendors participated. Afterwards, a transcript was posted to FedBizOpps along with the solicitation.
    - This strategy increased competition and resulted in a better solution using innovative ideas that had not previously been considered.
    - This virtual outreach can save time and money and increase participation.

To further assist agencies in these efforts, an Acquisition Collaboration Toolkit has been added to the "vendor engagement collaboration community of practice" at https://max.omb.gov/community/x/_INBIg. To facilitate their early communication with vendors, agencies have multiple tools at their disposal, ranging from wikis and blogs to webinars and meetings. The Acquisition Collaboration Toolkit provides tips, checklists, and additional information on how to use various media tools to host early vendor engagement opportunities. If you have additional best practices and success stories regarding ways to facilitate vendor collaboration, please send them to Joanie Newhart at the email address below.

More effective vendor engagement results from a change in culture in both government and industry organizations. Government professionals must incorporate vendor engagement strategies into their acquisition planning and execution whenever possible. Industry professionals should understand that agencies must balance their limited resources, and that expansion of vendor engagement must begin in those areas most likely to produce positive outcomes in the form of greater efficiency, contract savings, or better requirements development. Together, our efforts will result in more effective solutions to the government's needs and provide a better value proposition for all of us as taxpayers.

Thank you for your commitment to this important matter. Please contact Joanie Newhart on (202) 395-4821 or jnewhart@omb.eop.gov if you have any questions.

Attachment –Vendor Misconceptions about Communications with the Federal Government

cc:

Agency General Counsels and Solicitors
Agency Ethics Officers

Vendor Misconceptions about Communications with the Federal Government

1.	Misconception –"The best way to present my company's capabilities is by marketing directly to Contracting Officers and/or signing them up for my mailing list."
	Fact – Contracting officers and program managers are often inundated with general marketing material that doesn't reach the right people at the right time. As an alternative, vendors can take advantage of the various outreach sessions that agencies hold for the purpose of connecting contracting officers and program managers with companies whose skills are needed.

Contracting and program offices are often inundated with marketing material, and this fact lowers the chances that a vendor's reliance on marketing material will enable these offices to focus on the firm's capabilities.

A more effective approach is to make your capabilities known through outreach sessions that agencies hold to provide information on how best to do business with the agency, and to provide information on future requirements. Many times these outreach sessions will provide an opportunity for vendors to meet with program managers and contracting officials to generally discuss items on annual procurement plans. Vendors are also encouraged to attend pre-proposal conferences to receive more detailed information about specific agency requirements.

A new Vendor Collaboration Central Event Listing has been added to the FedBizOpps homepage, www.fbo.gov, which provides quick and easy access to agency vendor communication plans and upcoming vendor collaboration events or engagement opportunities, such as industry days, pre-RFP conferences, vendor forums, etc. The FedBizOpps homepage also has a Small Business Central Event Listing where agencies post small business events, such as conferences and training, which can also help you make contact with the appropriate individuals within an agency.

Being familiar with already-available information reduces the burden on the workforce generally, and will make your conversations more targeted and productive. There are several resources that are available to help you find information about existing contracts and upcoming projects. For example, www.usaspending.gov can be queried to get information about current contracts that may be expiring soon; agency websites often have their advanced acquisition forecasts posted,[4] and appropriations acts can be a good place to look to see what the agency plans to acquire in the coming year. Another resource is the Government Printing Office's (GPO's) Federal Digital System (FDSYS), available at http://www.gpo.gov/fdsys/. FDSYS has electronic copies of the U.S. Government Budget, Code of Federal Regulations, and other helpful information. To better understand agency market research practices, the Department of Homeland Security's Market Research Guide[5] details the process and can provide insight on how and why market research is conducted.

Best Practices

- *The Department of Homeland Security's (DHS) recent Industry Day was conducted via live webcast and was attended or viewed by nearly 2,700 vendors. The event, hosted by the Office of the Chief Procurement Officer (OCPO), provided a valuable opportunity for industry stakeholders to learn early in the acquisition process about the Department's acquisition goals and expectations and other matters that affect their ability to compete for contracts. In an effort to involve industry more in the outreach, DHS asked industry leaders to moderate the panel discussions and lead the questioning of DHS panelists about issues involving the top DHS spend categories -- professional services, science and technology, screening technology, and cyber security/intelligence. Industry's response to the new format and the event itself was overwhelmingly positive.*
- *The U.S. Agency for International Development (USAID) holds small business vendor outreach sessions that are posted on www.fbo.gov. At these sessions, USAID typically provides information on doing business with USAID, has a prime contractor discuss its current role in supporting the agency's mission and relief efforts overseas, and offers a small business success story.*

- *It's always a good idea for an agency to find out why vendors did not bid on a solicitation. It's worth taking the time to call the vendor in case there were competition-limiting items in the solicitation or practices in the acquisition process. Obtaining this information allows the agency to improve future acquisition processes.*
- *Agency contracting professionals do not find mass emails helpful as these professionals are frequently inundated with generic marketing materials. It is much more effective to target your e-mails to them on specific capabilities or projects.*

2.	Misconception – "It is a good idea to bring only business development and marketing people to meetings with the agency's technical staff."
	Fact – In meetings with government technical personnel, it's far more valuable for you to bring subject matter experts to the meeting rather than focusing on the sales pitch.

Agency personnel are interested in better understanding the marketplace, advances in technology, and your firm's capabilities. In order to gain this understanding, it is usually more helpful for them to discuss technical issues than business development issues.

Industry professionals can benefit by conducting research about the agency in advance of scheduled meetings with agency professionals. Valuable time during one-on-one meetings is often spent sharing commonly available information, which is not helpful to either party. Before meeting with agency personnel, review information on the agency's website, such as the agency's mission, structure and organization; its advanced acquisition plans; and its budget. In addition, information on existing contracts in your areas of interest is available at www.usaspending.gov, and information on the specific program of interest is at http://business.usa.gov/find-resources. This information will enable you to tailor your presentation to agency officials.

Your technical team may be in the best position to provide the information that the agency needs, and therefore they should be included in these meetings.

Best Practices

- *The Nuclear Regulatory Commission (NRC) has several avenues for industry outreach: 1) Quarterly Business Seminars which educate vendors about the agency, its mission and business opportunities, as well as NRC's technical programs, 2)Reverse Green Technology Fairs which feature one-on-one discussions between vendors and Project Managers regarding current technology and future IT requirements, and 3) One-on-One Technical Counseling Sessions which provide vendors with technical guidance on how to conduct business with NRC. Once a specific requirement opportunity is identified, a meeting is coordinated between the specific Project Manager and the vendor. NRC's Office of Small Business and Civil Rights facilitates these vendor outreach sessions.*

– *Vendors should bring their technical experts to meetings with agencies. Their knowledge of advances in technology and your firm's capabilities are much more helpful to agencies than generic sales presentations.*

3.	Misconception – "Attending industry days and outreach events is not valuable because the agency doesn't provide new information."
	Fact – Industry days and outreach events can be a valuable source of information for potential vendors and are increasingly being used to leverage scarce staff resources.

The purpose of industry days and outreach events is to communicate the agency mission and upcoming requirements to industry. This information will assist you in deciding whether to invest valuable resources in developing a bid or proposal in response to the government's solicitation requirements. Vendors may have the opportunity to hear from and speak to agency representatives about their requirements, and can often meet one-on-one with agency personnel before or after the event. Many times, agencies hold sessions designed to help new vendors do business with them. In these sessions, agency personnel are on hand to answer any questions about how to do business with the agency. Gaining a better understanding of an agency will help you more effectively target your outreach, thereby saving valuable resources, and helping you respond to solicitations more effectively. In addition, industry days are a great way to network and make potential subcontract contacts. The Vendor Collaboration Central Event Listing on the Federal Business Opportunities webpage (www.fbo.gov) can help you identify events being held.

Best Practices

- *More agencies are beginning to hold these meetings virtually to save time and money and increase competition. For example, the Department of Education held a webinar with prospective offerors in the presolicitation phase of the English Language Learners Professional Development Network procurement. This webinar was advertised in advance on FedBizOpps, and 55 vendors participated. Afterwards, a transcript was posted to FedBizOpps along with the solicitation. In addition, the new toolkit for increasing pre-RFP communication encourages agencies to use a variety of social media to engage vendors. If your travel dollars are limited, ask agencies to make their industry days more accessible by offering them online or using other, widely-accessible technologies.*
- *Agency events can be very valuable. Not only do vendors learn more about the agency, they also get a chance to talk to agency contracting and program professionals face-to face. Vendors should take advantage of agency outreach opportunities.*

4.	Misconception – "Agencies generally have already determined their requirements and acquisition approach so our impact during the pre-RFP phase is limited."
	Fact – Early and specific industry input is valuable. Agencies generally spend a great deal of effort collecting and analyzing information about capabilities within the marketplace. The more specific you can be about what works, what doesn't, and how it can be improved, the better.

Agencies appreciate industry's valuable input into their acquisition strategies and solicitation packages because it may result in a better solution to their requirements. Simply providing suggestions and comments prior to formal requirements development will not trigger an organizational conflict of interest, as long as the vendor is not then hired to develop the requirements. Suggesting detailed solutions to your concerns is even more valuable. Agencies may issue a Request for Information (RFI) as part of market research to investigate the industry and marketplace in accordance with Federal Acquisition Regulation (FAR) Part 10, to determine if commercial items are available, to determine if small businesses are capable of meeting the agency's needs, and for many other planning purposes. Agencies may also issue a draft RFP to obtain comments and suggestions from potential vendors on how to improve the solicitation. Agencies may hold pre-solicitation or pre-proposal conferences or webinars, or post wikis to explain the requirements, solicitation process, and evaluation factors.[6] These engagement opportunities often allow for vendor questions and feedback. You should take advantage of every opportunity to provide the kind of targeted suggestions you'd like to see in the finished product.

Additionally, FAR 15.201 encourages exchanges with all interested parties, beginning at the earliest identification of a requirement through receipt of proposals. After release of a solicitation, the contracting officer is the focal point of any communications with the government to ensure a fair competition is conducted. Many times, a question and answer period is included in the acquisition process, allowing time for potential offerors to review the solicitation and submit questions. Should that not be the case, you are still encouraged to ask the contracting officer any questions that you have, in a timely manner, in order to ensure you understand the solicitation. Contracting officers generally prefer questions via e-mail so that they can ensure they understand the question and so they can facilitate obtaining an answer. Should the contracting officer decide to make any changes to the solicitation, it will be done via an amendment to the solicitation and posted for public viewing.

Best Practices

- *In trying to get the best value for their agency and for the taxpayers, contracting and program professionals want to know when products or services are available in the marketplace that can save money or provide a better solution or both. It is most helpful to provide that information early in the procurement cycle.*
- *Be specific and clear in your feedback. For example, if an agency is considering a performance-based contract for services but, in your firm's view, has not adequately defined the performance standards, provide the agency with specific suggestions for how the work should be evaluated based on your experience and expertise.*
- *The General Services Administration's Central Contracting Office recently sought input on the procurement of the next generation of the agency's enterprise IT services and support. Through RFIs, the agency first sought input on the current challenges and strategic technology initiatives, asking industry how it would recommend the*

agency approach those challenges. A subsequent RFI was issued to seek more specific input to the draft solicitation. A pre-proposal conference, attended by over 50 vendors, helped to further refine agency requirements.

5.	Misconception – "If I meet one-on-one with agency personnel, they may share my proprietary data with my competition."
	Fact – Agency personnel have a responsibility to protect proprietary information from disclosure outside the Government and will not share it with other companies.

Agency personnel have a responsibility to protect any information that was received in confidence from an offeror. During source selection, the Procurement Integrity Act and its implementing provisions in the FAR[7] prohibit Federal procurement officials from disclosing – prior to award of the relevant contract – contractor bid, proposal information or source selection information to any person other than a person authorized to receive such information. Procurement officials take this prohibition very seriously; if a violation occurs, there may be criminal and civil penalties.

While the protections of the Procurement Integrity Act do not apply prior to source selection, other protections remain. In many cases, the Trade Secrets Act[8] will prohibit Federal employees from divulging protected information, including confidential commercial or financial data, trade secrets, operations, processes, or style of work. Also, the Freedom of Information Act (FOIA) allows agencies to protect commercial or financial information that is privileged or confidential.[9] In cases where a vendor is concerned that existing protections are insufficient and engaging in pre-solicitation communication will be beneficial, agencies should consider the use of appropriate non-disclosure agreements (NDAs) to ensure that proprietary information will be kept from potential competitors.

6.	Misconception – "Agencies have an obligation not to share information about their contracts, such as prices, with other agencies, similar to the obligation they have not to disclose proprietary information to the public."
	Fact – There are no general limitations on the disclosure of information regarding existing contracts between agencies within the Government. In fact, agencies are encouraged to share pricing information to ensure that we are getting the best value for our taxpayers.

As explained above, agencies have a responsibility to protect proprietary information from disclosure outside the Executive Branch. Restrictions on such outside disclosure prevent harm both to the competitive position of the contractor amongst its competitors and to the interest of the Government in being able to maintain a robust and competitive marketplace.

By contrast, the flow of information among and between agencies within the Executive Branch does not cause such harm. Moreover, such sharing among and between agencies can enable the Federal Government to root out wasteful duplication and negotiate better deals for the taxpayer.

Therefore, while there might be occasional circumstances where an agency could benefit from signing an NDA that would restrict its sharing of information with another agency, agencies should generally avoid NDAs that prohibit sharing of information – particularly pricing information – within the Government. Price visibility is critical to ensuring that the Government gets the best prices and that agencies are not paying more for the same products or services being bought under the same circumstances. As agencies face increasingly constrained budgets, it is critical that they share more pricing information with their Federal colleagues to ensure that the Federal Government is obtaining the best prices for the taxpayer.

Best Practice – GSA's SmartBuy Federal Strategic Sourcing Initiative (FSSI) provides a collaboration area for their interagency Commodity Team members to post their software orders and awarded contracts in order to share prices, and terms and conditions. This sharing of information will allow agencies to compare their requirements with those already procured by the Federal Government to ensure they get the best value for taxpayer dollars. Agencies are encouraged to participate in the Commodity Team. To request membership, send an e-mail to the SmartBuy team at smartbuy@gsa.gov.

7.	Misconception – "To develop my new proposal, I don't really need to tailor my solution to the specific solicitation since the government won't read my proposal that closely anyway."
	Fact – Offerors should tailor each proposal to the evaluation criteria, proposal instructions, and specific requirements of the solicitation to which they are responding. Contracting Officers and evaluation team members read proposals closely for compliance with the proposal instructions and must evaluate them against the evaluation factors and the statement of work in the solicitation.

Each proposal should be tailored to the final solicitation which lists the requirements, instructions to offerors on how to propose, and evaluation factors. Using your proposal, Government evaluators will determine the strengths and weaknesses of your proposal and also your firm's ability to perform the prospective contract successfully. If you cut and paste from previous proposals or repeat the solicitation, your proposal may miss the mark in explaining your solution. Offerors that are not responsive to the solicitation risk being eliminated from the competition, thereby wasting valuable time and resources used to prepare the proposal.

You should attend a pre-solicitation or pre-proposal conference if it is offered by the agency. At that conference, the agency will provide you with a better understanding of the procurement and what is required in the proposal, which will help you develop a more comprehensive proposal addressing the requirements.

If you are looking for some assistance in how to be most responsive to government solicitations, there are several resources available to assist you:

- *Business Breakthrough*: GSA has recently created this program to help businesses better understand how to successfully navigate government contracting, including strategies to prepare a winning proposal.[10]
- *Procurement Technical Assistance Program*: Created by Congress in 1985 to help businesses seeking to compete successfully in Federal, state and local government contracting, the nationwide network of Procurement Technical Assistance Centers provide one-on-one counseling sessions, classes, seminars and matchmaking events at little or no cost.[11]
- Offices of Small and Disadvantaged Business Utilization (OSDBU): OSDBUs are the primary advocate within each Federal executive agency responsible for promoting the maximum practicable use of all designated small business categories within the Federal acquisition process. You can find a listing of agency OSDBUs at http://www.osdbu.gov/members.html.
- Veterans First Contracting Program: The Department of Veterans Affairs has created the Center for Veterans Enterprise (CVE), which is solely dedicated to assisting veterans in starting and building businesses. CVE has a web portal for veteran-owned businesses which is available at http://www.vetbiz.gov.

- BusinessUSA.gov: A new website, BusinessUSA at http://business.usa.gov, was recently developed to be a one-stop shop to help small businesses and businesses of all sizes find information about available Federal programs and opportunities without having to spend time navigating from one Federal agency to another. BusinessUSA combines best practices and information from government agencies.

Best Practices

- *It is helpful to develop a checklist of solicitation requirements to ensure that a response is provided for each requirement and that it is in the format requested in the solicitation. If you follow the solicitation instructions, it will facilitate evaluation of your proposal.*
- *Proposals in which vendors simply cut and paste from the RFP or use the same language from a previous proposal often miss important evaluation factors or misunderstand the nuances of the requirements are rarely selected for award.*
- *Vendors should be fully responsive to all evaluation factors, including past performance information. Some vendors falsely assume they will get credit for good performance since the government was aware of its work, even if the vendor doesn't mention it in its proposal.*

8.	Misconception – "If I lose the competition, I shouldn't bother to ask for a debriefing. The Contracting Officer won't share any helpful information with me."
	Fact – Unsuccessful offerors should ask for a debriefing to understand the award decision and to improve future proposals.

In a formal procurement, the process by which offerors request and receive an explanation of the award decision is the debriefing. Asking for a debriefing is the best way to find out why you were not awarded the contract or order.

In accordance with FAR 15.505 and 15.506, agencies must provide debriefings to unsuccessful offerors in negotiated procurements upon written request either when excluded from the competitive range prior to award, or upon notification of award. These debriefings can be provided in person or in writing, depending on the agency's preference. When conducting competitions under FAR Part 8, agencies must provide a brief explanation to unsuccessful offerors on awards that are based on factors other than price alone. You can use the information provided to adjust your proposal strategy in future procurements to be more competitive.

We recognize that agencies can sometimes do a better job of letting vendors know why they didn't receive an award. This is especially true in cases where award is based on other than price alone. While agency procurement personnel are extremely busy, often handling multiple solicitations and contracts at the same time, OFPP's February 2, 2011 "Myth-Busting" memorandum encouraged agency contracting professionals to not only provide debriefs, but to provide as much information as possible in the debriefing.

Best Practices

- *One agency encourages the debriefing of the winning offeror. This way, the vendor can get specific, targeted feedback on what it did right in the proposal and what it could do even better in the future.*
- *Another agency writes its selection memorandum with detailed information about the strengths and weaknesses of all the offers so that everyone who bid can understand the outcome. This has reduced protests and received positive feedback from participants.*
- *Agencies appreciate when unsuccessful vendors request debriefings because it gives contracting professionals an opportunity to point out weaknesses in the vendor's proposal and provide them with the rationale for award. This valuable information can help vendors be more competitive on future proposals.*

End Notes

[1] The 25 Point Implementation Plan to Reform Federal Information Technology Management is available at http://cio.gov/documents/25-Point-Implementation-Plan-to-Reform-Federal%20IT.pdf

[2] The OFPP memorandum of February 2, 2011, is available at http://www.whitehouse.gov/ sites/default/files/omb/procurement/memo/Myth-Busting.pdf

[3] Nothing in this memorandum should be read to alter, or authorize violations of applicable ethics rules, procurement integrity requirements, or other statutes or regulations that govern communication and information sharing.

[4] A list of Federal agencies with links to their websites is available at http://www.usa.gov/directory/federal/index.shtml.

[5] Appendix I to the Department of Homeland Security Acquisition Manual, available at http://www.dhs.gov/xlibrary/assets/opnbiz/cpo hsam.pdf

[6] Government personnel can learn more about creating productive pre-RFP engagements in the Acquisition Collaboration Toolkit available on the vendor engagement collaboration community of practice at https://max.omb.gov/community/x/ INBIg.

[7] 48 C.F.R. § 3.104-1-11, available at http://www.gpo.gov/fdsys/pkg/CFR-2010-title48-vol1/pdf/CFR-2010-title48- vol1-part3.pdf

[8] 18 U.S.C. § 1905, available at http://www.law.cornell.edu/uscode/text/18/1905

[9] 5 U.S.C. § 552(b)(4), available at http://www.gpo.gov/fdsys/pkg/USCODE-2010-title5/pdf/USCODE-2010-title5- partI-chap5-subchapII-sec552.pdf

[10] More information is available at http://www.gsa.gov/portal/category/101431.

[11] More information is available at http://www.aptac-us.org/new/index.php.

In: Market Research
Editor: Cherese Hartell

ISBN: 978-1-63482-008-0

Chapter 4

OVERVIEW OF THE FEDERAL PROCUREMENT PROCESS AND RESOURCES*

L. Elaine Halchin

SUMMARY

In the basic federal procurement process, acquisition personnel, after determining their agency's requirements (that is, the goods and services the agency needs), post a solicitation on the Federal Business Opportunities (FedBizOpps) website. Interested companies prepare their offers in response to the solicitation, and, in accordance with applicable provisions of the Federal Acquisition Regulation (FAR), agency personnel evaluate the offers. Another type of procurement opportunity for a company is to serve as a subcontractor for a government contractor. To be eligible to compete for government contracts, a company must obtain a Data Universal Numbering System (DUNS) number and register with the federal government's System for Award Management (SAM). Several agencies, such as the General Services Administration (GSA), provide assistance and services to existing and potential government contractors. Research and development (R&D) procurement opportunities may involve traditional contracting methods, such as solicitations and contracts, as well as nontraditional methods, which include agency-sponsored contests and venture capital funds.

* This is an edited, reformatted and augmented version of a Congressional Research Service publication, CRS Report for Congress RS22536, prepared for Members and Committees of Congress, from www.crs.gov, dated September 11, 2012.

INTRODUCTION

The federal government's basic procurement or acquisition process involves an agency identifying the goods and services it needs (also known as the agency's "requirements"), determining the most appropriate method for purchasing these items, and carrying out the acquisition. Although this process is simple in theory, any given procurement can be complex, involving a multitude of decisions and actions.

A contracting officer may need to determine, for example, whether to use a federal supply schedule (see below), what type of contract to use, whether simplified acquisition procedures may be used, or whether the procurement should be set aside for small businesses.[1] Thus, this report does not attempt to describe every possible type of procurement. Instead, it describes the most common elements of the federal procurement process and resources that may be used in that process.

OVERVIEW OF FEDERAL GOVERNMENT PROCUREMENT

Federal Acquisition Regulation (FAR)

The primary source of federal procurement information and guidance is the *Federal Acquisition Regulation*, which consists of Parts 1-53 of Title 48 of the *Code of Federal Regulations* (CFR). Available at http://www.acquisition.gov/far, the FAR covers, for example, contractor qualifications, types of contracts, small business programs, and federal supply schedule contracting. The FAR also includes, in Part 2, definitions of procurement words and terms, and, in Part 52, solicitation provisions and contract clauses.

Eligibility Requirements for Businesses

With a few exceptions, a firm that wants to compete for federal government contracts must meet at least two requirements: (1) obtain a Data Universal Numbering System (DUNS) number, which is a unique nine-digit identification number for each physical location of a business, available at http://www.dnb.com/get-a-duns-number.html; and (2) register with the government's System for Award Management (SAM), at https://www.sam.gov. Additional requirements specific to a particular procurement may be found in the applicable solicitation (see below).

Summary of the Acquisition Process

Essentially, the federal acquisition process begins when an agency determines its requirements and how to purchase them. If the agency's contracting officer determines that the appropriate method for procuring the goods or services is a contract, and the contract amount is greater than $25,000, then the agency posts a solicitation on the Federal Business Opportunities (FedBizOpps) website, available at https://www.fbo.gov.[2] At a minimum, a solicitation identifies what an agency wants to buy, provides instructions to would-be offerors, identifies the source selection method that will be used to evaluate offers, and includes a deadline for the submission of bids or proposals.[3]

Agencies also may post solicitations on their own websites and, in exceptional circumstances, may post solicitations on their websites instead of on FedBizOpps. (The Federal Emergency Management Agency (FEMA) did this in the aftermath of Hurricane Katrina in 2005).[4]

Following the deadline for companies to submit their offers, agency personnel evaluate offerors' submissions, using the source selection method and criteria described in the solicitation.[5] Unless multiple suppliers or firms are needed, such as for a supply schedule, the agency awards a contract to one firm.

RESOURCES FOR BUSINESSES

Governmental Resources

Congressional Research Service (CRS)

The Congressional Research Service has a webpage, available at http://www.crs.gov/resources/ Pages/fed-business.html, which provides links to resources for businesses. Members of Congress may request to have the CRS page added to their websites by selecting "click to request this page" on the CRS webpage.

General Services Administration (GSA)

The General Services Administration is perhaps best known, in terms of contracting opportunities and resources, as the agency that maintains numerous supply schedules. A schedule is a list of goods and/or services provided by GSA-selected multiple vendors at varying prices. (Hence, these schedules are known as multiple award schedules (MAS).) Information about schedules, including guidance for how to get on a schedule, and a link to GSA's Vendor Support Center, are available at http://www.gsa.gov/schedules.[6] The process for getting on a schedule is similar to that for obtaining a government contract: GSA issues a solicitation for particular goods or services, companies submit offers in response, and then GSA evaluates the offers and awards contracts to multiple vendors for the same goods or services. Schedule solicitations are posted on FedBizOpps, and GSA also posts them on its website. The GSA solicitation page may be accessed by going to http://www.gsa.gov/portal/content/207509.

Minority Business Development Agency (MBDA)

The Minority Business Development Agency, which is part of the Department of Commerce and whose website is available at http://www.mbda.gov, was "created specifically to foster the establishment and growth of minority-owned businesses in America."[7] The agency's network of business development centers provides a variety of management and technical assistance services, and its Phoenix/Opportunity Matching System, a free online system, is designed to match entrepreneurs with federal government and private sector contracting opportunities.

Procurement Technical Assistance Program (PTAP)

Although the Procurement Technical Assistance Program is administered by the Defense Logistics Agency (DLA), it is available to assist companies that market products and services to all federal agencies, and state and local governments.[8] Services are provided through 94 Procurement Technical Assistance Centers (PTACs), which have over 300 local offices. To find PTACs, visit http://www.aptac-us.org/new/Govt_Contracting/find.php. The centers provide assistance through classes, seminars, and individual counseling sessions.[9]

Small Business Administration (SBA)

The Small Business Administration offers a variety of services and assistance to current and would-be government contractors. Its website, available at http://www.sba.gov, includes information on, among other topics, contract opportunities, online training, and laws and regulations. The SBA also offers training and counseling services through its Office of Entrepreneurial Development, available at http://www.sba.gov/about-offices-content/1/2463. This site includes, for example, information about Small Business Development Centers, which provide management and technical assistance to small businesses. Free online courses, on topics such as government contracting and marketing and advertising, also are available on the SBA website, at http://www.sba.gov/category/navigation-structure/counseling-training.[10]

Non-Governmental Resources

Other resources that firms may find useful in identifying procurement opportunities, navigating the government's procurement process, and marketing their goods or services include professional, trade, and industry organizations, publications, and events; local chambers of commerce; and consultants. For example, the book *Elements of Government Contracting*, by Richard D. Lieberman and Karen R. O'Brien, provides information about the federal procurement process. Magazines such as *Government Executive* and *Homeland Defense Journal* include articles with information about government procurements and industry workshops or conferences. Industry and trade organizations, such as the Professional Services Council, may be another source of useful information.[11]

Selected Topics

Research and Development Procurement

Part 35 of the FAR provides guidance on research and development (R&D) contracting. Interested companies, organizations, and other entities may use FedBizOpps to identify R&D opportunities, which may be posted as solicitations or broad agency announcements (BAA).[12]

The federal government also uses several nontraditional procurement methods to acquire the technologies and products it needs. Recognizing that not all new and innovative ideas may be captured by established procurement programs and procedures, the federal government provides for the submission of unsolicited proposals. That is, a firm may submit a proposal for which there is no solicitation. Guidance and requirements for the preparation and submission of unsolicited proposals, including the criteria for a valid unsolicited proposal, may be found at Subpart 15.6 of the FAR. Some agencies may also provide information on their websites about unsolicited proposals, which the Department of Homeland Security (DHS) does at http://www.dhs.gov/unsolicited-proposals.

As the central R&D organization for the Department of Defense, the Defense Advanced Research Projects Agency (DARPA) "was established ... to prevent strategic surprise from negatively impacting U.S. national security and create strategic surprise for U.S. adversaries by maintaining the technological superiority of the U.S. military."[13]

The DARPA website, available at http://www.darpa.mil/default.aspx, includes links to solicitations and BAAs, and a webpage dedicated to opportunities for small businesses, available at http://www.darpa.mil/Opportunities/SBIR_STTR/SBIR_STTR.aspx. The Department of Homeland Security (DHS) has an organization, the Homeland Security Advanced Research Projects Agency (HSARPA), that performs a similar function for DHS. Information about HSARPA and its funding opportunities is available at http://www.dhs.gov/st-hsarpa. The Technical Support Working Group (TSWG) is the "[n]ational interagency research and development program for combating terrorism requirements at home and abroad."[14] The working group uses the BAA Information Delivery Systems (BIDS), available at https://www.bids.tswg.gov/tswg/bids.nsf/Start?ReadForm&8EBQYZ, to post BAAs and collect proposals.

Other nontraditional opportunities for firms, research institutions, and organizations are government-sponsored contests and venture capital funds established by agencies for the purpose of helping to fund technologies the agencies could use. For example, the National Aeronautics and Space Administration (NASA) sponsors Centennial Challenges. Information is available at http://www.nasa.gov/offices/oct/early_stage_innovation/ centen nialchallenges/index.html.

Two agencies that have established venture capital funds are the Central Intelligence Agency (CIA) and the Department of the Army. Information about the nonprofit corporation that was established to manage the CIA's venture capital fund—In-Q-Tel—is available at http://www.iqt.org/. Information about OnPoint Technologies, the Army's venture capital fund, is available at http://www.onpoint.us/.

Subcontracting Opportunities

Another way to become involved in federal government contracting, albeit indirectly, is to serve as a subcontractor for a company (known as the "prime contractor") that has been awarded a government contract. Agencies may provide information on their websites about firms to which they have awarded contracts. For example, GSA maintains a subcontracting directory, available at http://www.gsa.gov/subdirectory, and DHS provides a list of prime contractors at http://www.dhs.gov/prime-contractors. Other potentially useful sources of information include trade and business publications, FedBizOpps, company websites, and the Federal Procurement Data System (FPDS).[15] Information gleaned from these sources might indicate which companies have received, or expect to receive, government contracts. The SBA provides information regarding subcontracting opportunities at http://www.sba.gov/category/navigation-structure/ contracting/contracting-opportunities/sub-contracting.

End Notes

[1] Information about these topics may be found in Parts 38 (federal supply schedules), 16 (types of contracts), 13 (simplified acquisition procedures), and 19 (small business programs) of the Federal Acquisition Regulation (FAR), which is discussed in the next section.

[2] Examples of procurement methods that do not involve establishing a new contract include using a government purchase card (that is, a credit card); placing a task order (or a delivery order) against an existing contract; or ordering from a GSA schedule (schedules are described in the next section of the report). The governmentwide commercial purchase card is, in effect, a credit card government employees may use to make certain types of purchases. It is known for being used to make micro-purchases, which are items that do not exceed the micro-purchase threshold of $2,500. For additional information, see FAR 2.101 and FAR Subpart 13.2. A delivery order (or task order) contract, which also may be known as an indefinite-delivery contract, is "a contract for supplies [or services] that does not procure or specify a firm quantity of supplies [or services] (other than a minimum or maximum quantity) and provides for the issuance of orders for the delivery of supplies [or the issuance of orders for the performance of tasks] during the period of the contract." (FAR 16.501-1.)

[3] An "offer" is a response to a solicitation. A company or individual who submits an offer is known as an "offeror."

[4] For information about Hurricane Katrina contracting, see CRS Report RS22280, Hurricane Katrina Recovery: Contracting Opportunities, by L. Elaine Halchin.

[5] The two primary categories of source selection are sealed bidding (FAR Part 14) and negotiated contracting (FAR Part 15).

[6] GSA offers several resources that target companies interested in selling their products or services on one or more schedules. The resources are available at http://www.gsa.gov/portal/category/100635. Another resource for businesses is GSA's forecast of contracting

opportunities, which is available at http://www.gsa.gov/portal/content/101163. To find GSA's training opportunities for vendors, visit http://www.gsa.gov/portal/content/203017.

[7] U.S. Department of Commerce, Minority Business Development Agency, "Who Is MBDA?" available at http://www.mbda.gov/main/who-mbda/who-mbda.

[8] Defense Logistics Agency, "What Is the PTAP?" available at http://www.dla.mil/Small Business/Pages/ptap.aspx.

[9] Association of Procurement Technical Assistance Centers, "Procurement Training," available at http://www.aptacus.org/new/Govt_Contracting/index.php.

[10] CRS has a number of reports on topics related to small businesses. The list includes, for example, CRS Report R41038, Survey of Federal Laws Containing Goals, Set-Asides, Priorities, or Other Preferences Based on Race, Gender, or Ethnicity, by Jody Feder, Kate M. Manuel, and Julia Taylor; CRS Report R40860, Small Business Size Standards: A Historical Analysis of Contemporary Issues, by Robert Jay Dilger; and CRS Report R40744, The "8(a) Program" for Small Businesses Owned and Controlled by the Socially and Economically Disadvantaged: Legal Requirements and Issues, by Kate M. Manuel and John R. Luckey.

[11] The mention of these particular publications and this group is not intended to be, and should not be construed as, an endorsement.

[12] A broad agency announcement is used "for the acquisition of basic and applied research and that part of the development not related to the development of a specific system or hardware procurement. BAA's may be used by agencies to fulfill their requirements for scientific study and experimentation directed toward advancing the state-of-the-art or increasing knowledge or understanding rather than focusing on a specific system or hardware solution." (FAR 35.016(a).)

[13] Defense Advanced Research Projects Agency, "Our Work," at http://www.darpa.mil/our_work/.

[14] Technical Support Working Group, "Technical Support Working Group," available at http://www.tswg.gov/. This text no longer is readily visible on http://www.tswg.gov, however, it remains as the Web page's meta description. A cached copy of the Web page displaying this text may be viewed at http://bit.ly/PalNzm.

[15] The Federal Procurement Data System, which is available at https://www.fpds.gov, includes information about government contract actions over $3,000. (FAR 4.602.)

INDEX